Essentials for *Food* Safety

Essentials for *Food* Safety

The Fight against Microorganisms

ROGER LEWIS

ESSENTIALS FOR FOOD SAFETY
THE FIGHT AGAINST MICROORGANISMS

iUniverse books may be ordered through booksellers or by contacting:

iUniverse
1663 Liberty Drive
Bloomington, IN 47403
www.iuniverse.com
1-800-Authors (1-800-288-4677)

Because of the dynamic nature of the Internet, any web addresses or links contained in this book may have changed since publication and may no longer be valid. The views expressed in this work are solely those of the author and do not necessarily reflect the views of the publisher, and the publisher hereby disclaims any responsibility for them.

Any people depicted in stock imagery provided by Thinkstock are models, and such images are being used for illustrative purposes only. Certain stock imagery © Thinkstock.

ISBN: 978-1-5320-1619-6 (sc)
ISBN: 978-1-5320-1618-9 (e)

Library of Congress Control Number: 2017904571

Print information available on the last page.

iUniverse rev. date: 11/09/2017

Introduction

*T*his is a stimulating book for those who have a passion for the food-and-beverage business and want to improve their knowledge in established and up-to-date cleaning and sanitation procedures.

Food safety is a vital part of our daily lives. It is essential for us to stay healthy, along with consuming the right foods that ensure we are energetic and strong and able to fight diseases and repair damage to cells. One of the greatest improvements in sanitation and health care over the years has been the enhancement of public health programs by the various health departments across the world that ensure we are provided with clean water for human and animal consumption, farming, food processing, restrooms, and other public areas. They also ensure strict food-safety standards for manufacturing and catering businesses that provide food for consumption and the improvement of health care facilities and processes.

Also of note is that food businesses must comply with established cleaning and sanitation procedures to reduce the risk of food-borne illnesses. A food-borne illness or food poisoning, according to the United States Centers for Disease Control and Prevention (CDC), is any illness caused by the consumption of contaminated foods or beverages. Many different disease-causing microbes, or pathogens, can contaminate foods, so there are many different food-borne infections. In addition, poisonous chemicals or other harmful substances can cause food-borne diseases if they are present in food, the CDC notes.[1]

Food safety should therefore not be taken lightly. Yet it is daily. Why? Sometimes we just don't know the correct procedure to get the results we desire. There is also a lack of training in institutions such as hospitals, hotels, and restaurants when it comes to food safety. This training may not take place because of some owners' or operators' lack of knowledge of the importance of food safety. Many times there is a lack of care and attention to the very important steps in the food chain by the operators, yet they insist on their establishments serving the best food and charging premium prices. That just doesn't seem like the best equation.

Just think about it. If you were dining in a restaurant and were able to see poor preparation and sanitation procedures in the food-handling process, you would most certainly not pay for the meal; neither would you return to that establishment ever again. Furthermore, as a dissatisfied customer, you would spread a negative message about the restaurant, which would discourage others from patronizing that business.

Too often, owners of food establishments leave themselves totally exposed to food-borne illnesses that can lead to lawsuits and bad reputations because they refuse to follow the principles of food safety, even after pumping hundreds of thousands and even millions of dollars into their businesses.

There are many instances in which sanitation is the first area targeted when there is a need to cut costs. Why? Sanitizing food-preparation equipment is vital to eliminating the various bacteria and viruses from the utensils and cutlery that we use to consume our meals.

---

[1] http://www.cdc.gov/foodsafety/foodborne-germs.html

Too often, proprietors wait until a situation is critical before trying to fix it, by which time much has been lost. In this line of business, you really don't get a second chance to make a great impression. The food business is unforgiving. Once something goes wrong, it takes years to fix, particularly your reputation.

Eating is a very personal and intimate experience. Your body is very sensitive to what you put in it, and your taste buds and sense of smell can, in most instances, detect food that is not fresh or properly prepared.

Today there is a new drive in sanitation because of the many problems that bacteria and viruses cause. These microorganisms can make us very sick and, in some cases, even cause death. This is where a proper sanitation program comes into play. Proper hygiene also prolongs the shelf life of various foods, fruits, vegetables, and meats.

In the food business, it takes months to earn a good customer and just seconds to lose him or her. Customers today are very aware of where and what they eat, and in this information age, they are constantly educating themselves to ensure they get the best total value for their money. Eateries owe it to the public and their regular customers to provide them with clean and sanitary environments, utensils, and food-preparation areas and great food through an established cleaning-and-sanitation program.

Thank you for choosing this book for training. The topics discussed in this book will serve as a great refresher for you in the very important process of serving food safely and keeping your customers returning to your business. Remember—repeat business is the key to your success.

The information outlined in this guidebook does not cover all the areas in the food-safety chain for commercial, institutional kitchens and food-preparation areas. The author offers no guarantee or warranty; nor does he accept liability for environmental hazards, food poisoning, production loss or costs, health issues, or lawsuits. This guidebook does not endorse any company's products, practices, or procedures.

About the Author

$\mathcal{I}$ have trained people and businesses in food safety for more than twenty years, and I have seen many things done incorrectly—from the approach to the customer to the delivery of the plate on the table. Customers don't always tell you about their bad experiences, but they will likely just never return and tell other people about those experiences. Social media networks and websites like TripAdvisor are new places for laying complaints and expressing dissatisfaction for the whole world to see.

I have also spent twelve years in electrical engineering, specializing in refrigeration and air-conditioning. Refrigeration is a very important part of food safety. Imagine the food business without it. Certainly we would have tremendous problems with spoilage and other serious complications in the food-safety process.

I have worked in the safety business for six years. Safety in every area is essential. It is crucial for your staff and customers as well. It is very important to provide the personal protective equipment needed to get the various tasks done effectively and safely. Employee safety is a major concern for many businesses and workers unions across the world today. Employers must be in compliance with local and, in some cases, international law. Safety for the guest is paramount. Not only are they demanding good food, but they are insisting on improved dining standards, and the pressure is on.

Why Have a Food-Safety Program

*T*he primary reason for a food-safety program is to prevent, reduce, and control any type of contamination, whether it is chemical, physical, or biological. This can be done through control programs aimed at preventing the entry of all forms of contamination. These focus on the receiving areas, proper storage, hygiene, and cooking and cooling temperatures, which are all critical control points. These critical points form part of the food-safety program called the Hazard Analysis of Critical Control Points (HACCP).

The National Advisory Committee on Microbiological Criteria for Foods states that the HACCP consists of seven principles:[2]

1. Conduct a hazard analysis.
2. Determine critical control points (CCPs).
3. Establish critical limits.
4. Establish monitoring procedures.
5. Identify corrective actions.
6. Verify that the system works.
7. Establish procedures for record keeping and documentation.

These steps are used to set up a HACCP plan, which is used to control risk, whether biological, physical, or chemical, in the flow of food and to reduce, prevent, and eliminate hazard to a safe level in the entire operation.

The HACCP plan must be a written, well-constructed document that is specific to the property or facility and remains unique to its equipment, operation, menu, customers, and the various processes.

All seven steps must be followed, as each is linked to ensure all critical points are covered and documented. Develop your plan as outlined in the following steps:

Steps 1–2

- Check your facility for hazards and decide what the CCPs are.
- Take a closer look at how the food is being processed. Many foods are processed similarly. Some foods are prepared and cooked the same day—for example, sandwiches and fresh salads—while others are prepared the previous day. Examine your cooking, holding, cooling, reheating, and serving.
- Review all your processes for all foods that are prepared similarly. Identify foods that need temperature control for

---

[2] http://www.fda.gov/Food/GuidanceRegulation/HACCP/ucm2006801. htm#princ

safety (TCS). You must determine what food items would be hazards in the process. Take note of the various hazards and determine if it is a CCP in the process. Where hazards are found, a new approach must be taken to eliminate them altogether or reach an acceptably safe level. In most cases, there is more than one CCP.

Steps 3–5

- Find ways to set control limits to monitor and decide what you will do to reduce or prevent a hazard.
- Implement limits by time, temperature, and procedure within which foods can be kept safe.
- With the new limits in place, using trained designated food handlers, check to ensure that the food is within the critical limits for food safety. Various foods have different times and frequency for checking. This is a good time to take records.
- If a critical limit is not met, identify and take step(s) to determine why it was not met. Thereafter, train and implement the revised or new limit.

Steps 6–7

- Make sure the plan is effective for the intended purpose and keep records of the various HACCPs.
- Evaluate the plan to ensure it is working as intended and meets established procedures. Check the process on a regular basis for effectiveness. Take notes and populate your charts with information of the various steps in the HACCP process to determine if the plan meets the principles of HACCP.
- If the plan is working, maintain the plan and secure all information that created the program. Records of the following actions must be kept: equipment condition; corrective action taken; activity monitoring; work with reputable supplier(s); temperatures; and time.

- Set up a daily checklist for all the items on the HACCP list. The manager, in conjunction with the supervisor, should control this list to record all the processes checked and met daily. Any corrective action must also be noted. The supervisor on duty must sign this important information, and the manager should review. Records should be kept for a minimum of one year.

Employee Safety

*F*ocusing on occupational health and safety is the first and most important step in making the working environment conducive and safe for producing good food. The layout of the food-preparation areas and the flow of food are very important. A properly laid out kitchen is key to many important aspects of the operation.

A.

Flames are often in food-preparation areas, and without care and attention, hot oil, grease, or gas leaks can easily spark a fire. Fire suppression systems and fire extinguishers must therefore always be in place and ready for use at any time. A reputable safety company should service these systems and extinguishers quarterly. It's important to note that there are different types of fire extinguishers for different types of fires. Your fire safety supplier can identify the required extinguishers for your establishment. Also note that all safety systems must be in compliance with local safety laws.

B.

Fire blankets are essential and should be located and properly installed near the hot side of the kitchen near the grills, stove, and hot air exhaust. These are vital for controlling and extinguishing grease fires. Never use water to extinguish a grease fire. When water is poured onto a grease fire, it vaporizes into steam almost instantaneously because of the intense heat. The water expands and forces the fire above it upward, creating huge flames.

C.

The exhaust hood should have a fire suppression system set up by a reputable fire safety company. The said company should also service these systems at the required scheduled dates. Grease buildup from cooking and grilling can cause a serious fire that can be very difficult to control if your fire suppression system is malfunctioning. You can lose your entire property if you don't have the right chemicals to extinguish a grease fire.

D.

All staff should have access to the various types of gloves needed in the operations. High-temperature gloves for the hot side are usually heavily padded to reduce heat transfer. High-temperature gloves can be made of neoprene, which prevents heat transfer up to 450 degrees Fahrenheit.

 Low-temperature gloves are for use in refrigeration, particularly in the freezer compartment. Items can be very cold, and the handling and processing can be challenging. You must also remember to have your jacket and boots as well.

Pay close attention to the changing of gloves in the food-preparation areas, such as the bakery, cold preparation, butchery, and so forth, as lack of compliance with proper safety procedures can result in cross-contamination. Gloves should be discarded when you move from handling one type of food to another; touch areas that are not sanitized; return from a break; talk on the phone; shake someone's hand; or notice they are torn. In the latter case, it is best to find any pieces that have broken off to ensure they are properly disposed of. If you are doing a specific task, such as making sandwiches, preparing meat, cutting vegetables, gloves must be changed every three hours to reduce the risk of cross-contamination.

G.

Aprons, hairnets, safety glasses, goggles, and so forth, should always be available for kitchen personnel. Some jobs do require the use of personal protective equipment (PPE) because of potential dangers, such as strong chemicals for heavy-duty degreasing that could splash or spill and cause injury to staff. Everything must be done to avoid accidents.

H.

Wearing clean and tidy uniforms are also a very important part of a food-safety program. This prevents cross-contamination from food soils on dirty uniforms. It's always best to change uniforms if the one you are wearing is soiled. This will certainly improve overall appearance, particularly for those working in the dining area, and it also serves as good personal hygiene.

I.

Safety footwear in the back of the house is absolutely essential. Many accidents happen in this area because staff, in many cases, is issued the wrong type of safety shoes. Many types of safety shoes are available, but how do you know which are the right ones for your team? There are different specifications for various types of safety shoes: construction safety shoes, electrician safety shoes, welder safety shoes, and so forth. For the food-and-beverage and back-of-the-house operations, the specs are nonslip, antistatic, waterproof, six-inch-high boots. It is also important to choose safety footwear a size over your normal shoe size and pair them with thick socks. This will allow for free movement when walking, bending, and standing for long periods of time. Diabetic persons should only use nonmetallic tip safety shoes to ensure they don't cause any damage to their feet. Some diabetics may only want to wear a strong, nonsafety shoe. This is acceptable in most cases.

The correct type of floor finish in the work area is essential for ensuring staff can move around safely. While certain kinds of floors may be attractive, they may not be practical for the work environment. The situation is made worse if the floor is wet and the surface becomes slippery and dangerous, providing the ideal circumstances for accidents to occur, which can result in leaves of absence, back injuries, cuts, bruises, and lawsuits. Extra care must be taken in these areas. A nonslip, grout-free surface is best.

Emergency eyewash stations should also be part of the safety setup. There will be accidents at some point in time, and systems must be in place to cope with unforeseen events. Emergency eyewash stations should be installed in sensitive areas such as the receiving area and the chemical storeroom.

L.

First-aid and burn kits should be located in the same areas. Remember that in emergency cases speed is crucial.

In the event there is a need for a quick evacuation, emergency exits must be accessible and clear of obstacles at all times. Do not stack or store items in or around these exits. Emergency exits should always have lighting and battery backup for use during a power failure, as persons would need to get to a safe area or cluster point. In an emergency, staff must follow the emergency exit procedures of the establishment.

Install reflective tape leading to emergency exits to guide staff to the exits in the event of a power failure.

Chemical Safety

$\mathcal{I}$n the day-to-day operation of any food-and-beverage department, cleaning and sanitation chemicals will be required. It is therefore essential that you and your team clearly understand a few simple but very important safety rules for using these products in food safety; the degreasing process for hood ranges, grills, pots, and pans; the process for cleaning floors and dish machines; and so forth. As we continue in this book, how these products should be applied and used will be clearly outlined.

All cleaning with chemicals requires awareness on the part of the user to ensure proper use and create a safe environment. Correct storage, handling, and use of the cleaning chemicals are very important for safety in the workplace. Products should also be used in compliance with your local health and safety laws, along with your supplier's procedural and safety instructions. Use products as the supplier directs, as failure to comply may result in serious hazards to you or others nearby, the surfaces, and the environment.

Some safety rules are listed below.

Always read the instructions carefully before using products. Most suppliers have adequate information on or in the product packaging for the correct care and handling procedures for the product.

Never mix chemicals, as this can cause violent chemical reactions, which can be very dangerous. Chemical reactions include but are not limited to the release of toxic gases; explosion; and an increase in heat that could rupture the product's container and cause damage to people or surfaces. Mix chemicals with water only.

The correct labels must always be on the various products. This is very important as you may have many people working in an area and you want to ensure that employees don't use the wrong product that could cause irreversible damage to surfaces and cause skin, eye, or respiratory problems. In some countries, there are fines for not having the correct labeling of containers when health and safety inspections are taking place.

Wear your PPE (personal protective equipment) at all times when you are in contact with cleaning products. In most cases, the container label will indicate the correct type of PPE needed for you to protect yourself.

Mop up spills right away and place the Wet Floor sign in the appropriate area to prevent slips and falls.

Never dose hazardous chemicals by hand. Skin can be severely damaged. Your chemical supplier can provide dispensers to mix and control the products.

Never handle hazardous chemicals with bare hands, as skin can be severely damaged. Your chemical supplier can provide dispensers to mix and control the products.

Use dispensers, where applicable, to ensure proper mixing ratios for products. Products mixed incorrectly can cause damage to surfaces, leave chemical residue on food contact surfaces, and be harmful to the user and the environment.

Carefully follow the important safety steps when changing a chemical container to prevent accidents.

Never transport a chemical without its lid in place. Products can splash and cause damage to the handler, others nearby, or property.

Following these safety guidelines can enhance your work environment. Reputable chemical suppliers will provide training on their products to ensure you and your team are well aware of the product's application and safety regulations.

Material safety data sheets (MSDSs) are very important for the use of chemicals in the operation. Your chemical supplier must supply a MSDS for all products delivered to the operation. The information consists of a list of very important information about each product, and no one in the establishment should use any products without proper training and reading the MSDS.

The MSDS contains information on dealing with spills, other safety precautions, the active ingredients and composition of chemicals, emergency response information, and storage information.

Personal Hygiene

$\mathscr{P}$ersonal hygiene is vital to food safety. The Centers for Disease Control and Prevention says a common cause of the spread of food-borne illnesses is food-safety personnel not washing their hands properly.[3] It estimated that millions of people get food poisoning yearly because food-preparation personnel do not follow an established hand hygiene program. Often food personnel are in a hurry, and they don't take the time to carry out the simple, yet very important, step of handwashing. This is critical for the success of a good food-safety program. Ensure there are adequate handwashing stations and hand soap.

Good practices start at home before you leave for work. A good shower is absolutely essential before going to work. Remember that our skin, hair, and mouth carry all types of bacteria, and a good shower will remove large amounts of those bacteria. All staff must also practice good hygiene habits on the job. Constant handwashing is vital to reducing cross-contamination and the spread of food-borne illnesses. There is a simple yet effective procedure.

[3] https://www.cdc.gov/nceh/ehs/ehsnet/plain_language/food-worker-handwashing-food-preparation.htm

Washing Your Hands the Right Way

Eight Steps to Handwashing

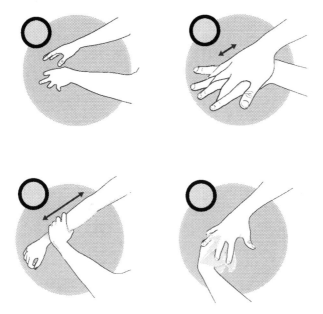

Hands should be washed up to the point where your shirtsleeve ends. Go to a handwashing sink, turn on water, wet your hands, and then dispense soap. Wash your hands vigorously with the antibacterial or antimicrobial hand soap and water for a minimum of twenty seconds from your fingertips to your elbows, between fingers, and the back and palm of the hands. Pay close attention to your nails. You can use a nailbrush to get under your nails. Fingernails must be clipped low to prevent food and soils from accumulating under them. Rinse in clean, warm water. Dry with a paper towel, and use a paper towel to turn off the tap. It's more hygienic to have a handwashing sink with a foot pedal or sensor so there is no need to use your hands to turn on or off the tap.

Handwashing Station

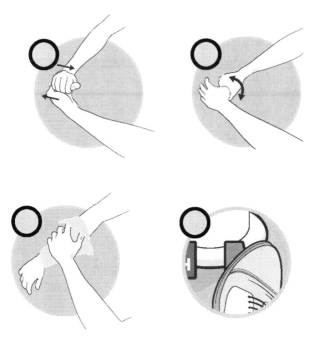

Always wash your hands after coughing, sneezing, eating, drinking, using the restroom, taking a smoke or coffee break, or touching your mouth or hair. Wash your hands between handling raw and cooked foods and between handling different raw foods. Clean your hands after changing from one food to another, handling money, or taking a phone call.

Not adhering to these handwashing rules can result in contamination of foods and can make people sick. There are many instances where food handlers easily make a guest very sick because they don't wash their hands in the situations listed previously.

It is very important that handwashing stations are installed throughout the kitchen in strategic locations to encourage proper handwashing. Each department should have its own handwashing station. It is also very important to have wall charts installed at handwashing stations and throughout the operation on the necessity of and correct procedures for proper handwashing.

A hand sanitizer is a good option for sanitizing your hands in between washes. However, this must not and cannot replace proper handwashing. This will kill 99.9 percent of all germs on your hands. The correct concentration of alcohol must be between 35 and 70 percent. It's a great practice to have hand sanitizer installed at the various entrances to the kitchen, in the various departments, and outside the restrooms.

Food-Borne Illness

*W*hat is a food-borne illness? Food-borne illness can be something as simple as diarrhea and vomiting or a severe sickness that can cause death. The World Health Organization (WHO) estimates that as many as 600 million, or almost 1 in 10 people in the world, fall ill after consuming contaminated food.[4]

Some of the common symptoms are headaches, dehydration, dizziness, abdominal pains, cramps, fever, and blurred vision. Usually these symptoms manifest at the early stage of food poisoning, and the severity depends on how much of the food one has consumed, how contaminated the food is, and what the contaminant is. It also depends on the strength of an individual's immune system.

The most common causes of food-borne illness are poor sanitation in food-handling areas; contaminated food utensils, food-preparation areas, and food equipment; biological hazards like bacteria, viruses, and parasites; and poor hygiene. Care and attention must be taken to clean and, most importantly, sanitize daily all aforementioned areas before preparing food.

---

[4] http://www.who.int/mediacentre/news/releases/2015/foodborne-disease-estimates/en/

At the end of the night shift, after you close and secure your business, pests can walk across the food-preparation areas. They can also leave droppings and urine, and these deposits can be so small we don't recognize them. At the beginning of each day, you must first pay close attention to the work areas, sanitizing them.

Food safety is so important that any case traced to your business can cause irreversible damage to the business's reputation. It can hurt profitability, and sometimes closure is inevitable. Following the strictest food-safety guidelines will ensure you and your food-preparation personnel do everything possible to avoid those types of damaging experiences.

Food Contaminants

Food must be safe from the growing and/or manufacturing process to consumption. Various steps must be followed to prevent food from becoming contaminated. Unsafe foods pose a global threat. Whether the causes are biological, chemical, or otherwise, unsafe food can be blamed for more than two hundred diseases, ranging from diarrhea to cancer, and can also lead to death.

According to the WHO, there were an estimated 582 million cases of 22 different food-borne enteric disease and 351,000 associated deaths in 2015. Salmonella was the main enteric disease agent, responsible for 52,000 deaths. E. coli was accountable for 37,000 deaths, and norovirus was responsible for 35,000 fatalities. Of those people suffering from disease caused by contaminated food, 40 percent were children under the age of five. The areas most burdened with diseases caused by contaminated food were the African region and Southeast Asia.

Germany's E. coli outbreak reportedly caused $1.3 billion (USD) in losses for farmers and another $236 million (USD) in emergency aid payments. Those huge costs and penalties occurred as a result of people and systems violating a part of the food chain.[5] Sanitation is a key component in the entire process of delivering safe food to your plate.

Foods are transported long distances from farms on trucks, trains, and so forth, to be delivered to cities where they are kept in cold storage, supermarkets, schools, and large catering and manufacturing companies. The journey can take days and even weeks. From the farm, foods must be well washed, rinsed, and sanitized to be good for consumption when they reach their final destination. If established food-safety practices are not adhered to, farmers can find themselves in serious problems with spoilage and large financial losses. They could possibly make people sick. All foods that ship out to various places across the world must meet international food-safety standards.

Microorganisms are small living organisms that are only visible through a microscope. Knowing how they grow and contaminate foods will help you to understand how to prevent food-borne illnesses. The harmful microorganisms are called pathogens. They include bacteria and fungi.

Bacteria

Bacteria are a major concern in the food business as they can cause serious problems in your operation if cleaning and sanitation guidelines are not observed. Bacteria can destroy raw and cooked food, making your customers very sick. They usually spread through poor hand hygiene, contaminated food, and dirty food utensils. Bacteria are single-cell organisms, and they live everywhere: in our skin, hair, mouth, nose, throat, intestine, and so forth. When your hands are contaminated, it is very easy to sully foods and preparation areas.

Certain foods allow bacteria to grow easily if not stored at correct temperatures. There are very important steps to follow to prevent foot spoilage and persons becoming sick. Some food products that break

---

[5] http://www.who.int/mediacentre/news/releases/2015/food-safety/en/

down easily because of bacterial growth are milk and milk products, poultry, pork, lamb, seafood and beef, sliced melon, and cantaloupe.

Bacteria only need four hours in the temperature danger zone (TDZ)—between 40 degrees Fahrenheit to 140 degrees Fahrenheit—to thrive, reproduce, and cause illnesses. The affected foods are mainly carbohydrates (starches) and proteins (sugars).

Bacteria commonly found in food operations are:

- Salmonella: associated with poultry
- Clostridium botulinum: associated with canned foods and vacuum-sealed packaging
- E. coli: associated with beef and leafy greens
- Listeria: associated with unpasteurized milk and processed meats
- Staphylococcus ureus: associated with workers who have cuts, boils, wounds, or sores on their skin.

Care and attention must be paid to these broken areas by either moving the worker to nonfood contact areas and treating and covering the damaged skin or sending the worker home until he or she gets better.

Viruses

Viruses are the leading cause of food-borne illnesses. They can contaminate water and food. They can be transmitted from person to person, from people to food, and from people to food-preparation areas. They can survive freezing and refrigeration. They cannot grow in food, but once eaten, they grow in your digestive system.

When a customer gets sick from food contaminated with a virus, in most cases, it's because the food handler has a virus. People who handle food should take several steps to avoid passing on viruses. They should wash hands often and avoid food contact with bare hands. All sick food handlers should stay away from work, particularly if they have gastroenteritis, vomiting, jaundice, and diarrhea.

Fungi

Fungi mostly spoil foods. They are found in the air, soil, and water.

Mold

Mold grows in most conditions but prefers acidic settings. Some molds produce toxins. Refrigeration will slow their growth but not kill them. Throw away all moldy food unless it is a natural part of the food.

Yeast

Yeast shares the same characteristics as mold. Yeasts spoil food rather quickly and leave a smell of alcohol. They usually have a white or pink coloration. They also grow well in acidic conditions. Throw out yeast-spoiled foods.

Food Allergens

Some people are allergic to certain foods—for example, nuts, dairy products, fish, soy products, wheat, eggs, and egg products. It is important to describe dishes to your customers who have food allergens. Also use separate oil to cook foods with allergens.

Foods that trigger allergic reactions can either affect people quickly or hours after consumption, and they have the potential to result in death. Symptoms of allergic reactions include tightening of the throat, hives, shortness of breath or wheezing, itching around face and mouth, loss of consciousness, swollen eyes or feet, cramps, diarrhea, and vomiting.

If a customer has an allergic reaction, call the emergency number in your area. Stay with the person, and always complete a report of the situation for your records.

Below are the top ten food-safety violations, as identified by Food Safety Violations author, Cindy Rice.[6]

1. Improper cooling of foods
2. Improper handwashing
3. Improper cold holding temperatures
4. Contaminated food contact surfaces and equipment
5. Improper labeling
6. Not labeling commercial containers
7. Failure to separate raw and cooked food
8. Improper reheating of food
9. Not maintaining hot holding temperature
10. Hand contamination of ready-to-eat food

Water

Water is the most important solvent on earth, and we can hardly do anything without it. Our bodies consist of over 70 percent water.

There are many differences in the quality of water across the world, and it is very important to have a basic understanding of the water you use in your area. The local laboratories in the areas you work can do water analysis for various properties. Potential contaminants in water may be microbial, chemical, or physical. Microbial contaminants are of the greatest concern, even though all contaminants cause health problems. Water used for drinking, food processing, and sanitizing must meet safe drinking water requirements in the country you are in.

You need to have good quality water in order to have good sanitation and great results in food quality. Water hardness is one of the key terms you must understand. That is the amount of minerals such as calcium (lime) and magnesium dissolved in the water, or total dissolved solids (TDS). These are headaches for the stewarding department, for example. Lime will deposit on food-processing equipment, glassware,

---

[6] https://foodsafety.ecolab.com/us/food-safety/Generic2?storeId=10154&catalogId=3074457345616698718&contentName=food-safety-matters/fsm-home

flatware, utensils, and plates, leaving a white cast that can make them look dirty and unsanitary. Using hard water in the operation leaves calcium deposits that are unsightly, smelly, and challenging to remove. A chemical descaler is the only way you will be able to remove the calcium buildup. However, it will redeposit on all the surfaces in a short space of time if you continue to use the same quality water. The descaling process will therefore have to be carried out repeatedly to keep the lime buildup under control. This can be quite costly and time-consuming, and it is not good for the environment.

Titrating or testing the water to determine the content is the first step to addressing this problem. This will reveal the levels of TDS and other impurities in the water. Remember—there may be microorganisms in the water, and a lab must test the water to establish the content of microorganisms. Your chemical supplier, however, can do titration.

Your chemical supplier can also do TDS tests, and the acceptable amount should be no more than 500 units parts per million (ppm), a unit of concentration commonly used as a measure of small levels of pollutants in water, air, and so forth.

The best water range for great results and spotless plates, glassware, equipment, and surfaces is soft water (0.2–4 grains per gallon [gpg], a unit of water hardness defined as one grain [64.8 milligrams] of calcium carbonate dissolved in one US gallon of water).

If the water received by the establishment is hard water, you will have to install a water-softening system to achieve the pristine results obtained by using soft water. Many companies offer these services. They will size the system for you based on your daily water consumption and the size of your water supply line.

With the water softener in place, there will be a huge improvement in not only the appearance of equipment and utensils and the level of calcium buildup but the taste of beverages as well. You can save on chemical consumption by over 15 percent, as there will be fewer impurities in the water to consume the chemistry.

If lab testing reveals harmful microorganisms in the water supply, a reputable lab may advise you to install a water filtration system that is designed to filter hazardous organisms. However, this is usually only necessary in extreme cases. Most water supply systems do treat the water, mainly with chlorine, to kill a broad spectrum of microorganisms. But it's best to carry out your own testing, depending on where you are.

Microorganisms found in water supplies include:

- Water pathogens: salmonella, shigella, pathogenic strains of E. coli (e.g., O157:H7), vibrio, Heliobacter, Yersinia, campylobacter
- Viruses: norovirus, enterovirus, hepatitis A, rotavirus
- Parasites: giardia, crytosporidium, cyclospora, amoeba, toxoplasma, roundworms, flatworms, tapeworms, Anabaena, rotifer, copepod, legionella

Chemicals such as pesticides, nitrates, mercury, lead, and so forth, can be found in water in large enough quantities to cause a health and environmental problem. Water from the municipal supply should be checked at least two to four times a year. Water from other sources should be tested monthly, and if there is other equipment in place for water treatment (chlorinator, ozone, etc.), it should be tested daily. It is always best to protect your investment and your customers.

Acidic and basic (alkaline) are two extreme properties of chemicals. A substance that is neither acidic nor alkaline—for example, pure water—is neutral. However, when chemicals are mixed with water, the mixture can become either acidic or alkaline. Examples of acidic substances are vinegar and lemon juice. Milk of magnesia and ammonia are examples of alkaline substances. Acids and alkaline substances have different purposes in cleaning and sanitation in the food-and-beverage industry.

The pH scale measures how acidic or alkaline a substance is by measuring the activity of hydrogen ions in it. The pH scale ranges from 0 to 14. A pH of 7 is neutral. A pH less than 7 is acidic. A pH greater than 7 is alkaline.

The pH scale is logarithmic, and as a result, each whole pH value below 7 is ten times more acidic than the next higher value. For example, pH 4 is ten times more acidic than pH 5 and 100 times (*10 x 10*) more acidic than pH 6. The same holds true for pH values above 7, each of which is ten times more alkaline than the next lower whole value. For example, pH 10 is ten times more alkaline than pH 9 and a hundred times (*10 x 10*) more alkaline than pH 8.

The scale below is an example of a pH scale.

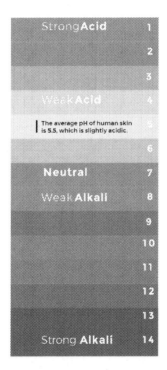

Mixing acids and alkaline substances can cancel out or neutralize each other's extreme effects. This can also be very dangerous, as in many cases harmful gases may be released, and the mixture can give off heat and melt the container.

Alkaline solutions are the main products used in cleaning. Degreasers for hoods and grills are usually strongly alkaline, and PPE (personal protective equipment) must be worn when handling strong degreasers.

Acids are used for descaling equipment that has calcium buildup. They are also used to remove iron stains that may come from the water supply.

The Receiving Area

*A*ll food establishments should have an area designated for the delivery of all goods. This is essential, as that area is the entry point for most food and nonfood items entering the property. Too often, this important area is not set up correctly so those persons receiving the goods can inspect them.

The receiving area is like the immigration area you pass through when you are entering another country. For example, the United States has strict rules and regulations that are enforced by highly trained staff who are equipped to identify those persons who do not meet the criteria of US immigration laws.

These immigration officers question you and check your history to determine if you will be allowed into the country. These officers have the power to reject your application for entry to their country, and they exercise that power if you do not meet immigration requirements, that is, if you have a criminal record, are a terrorist or drug lord, overstayed during your last visit, and so forth.

Similarly, the receiving officer and department at your establishment should operate on the same principles. He or she should determine what is allowed into the operation. For sure certain laws and conditions are very important and must be met in order for foods and other products to get the stamp of approval.

Sometimes receiving officers are not properly trained; neither do they have the equipment to carry out this very important job. They are often thrown in at the deep end with nothing but a computer and a desk and told to place orders with anybody who supplies goods at the best price.

This job requires far more respect and resources. This is a powerful position, just like the men or women in customs or immigration. Your establishment should take pride in the person you choose as your gatekeeper and train and equip the individual with all the tools necessary to get the job done properly and safely.

Remember he or she is taking care of your guest, your customers, and people you want to visit your hotel, restaurant, manufacturing plant, deli, and so forth. Why leave your investment at such a great risk?

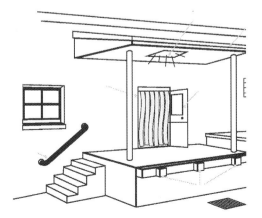

The individual who fills the role of food receiving officer must ensure that proper food-safety procedures are adhered to. Below are key areas that he or she would pay special attention to, to meet established food-safety standards.

A. A good food receiving officer should have a basic knowledge of food safety. This would greatly assist in the examination and refusal or acceptance of various food products.

B. The receiving area should always be clean and clear of traffic.

C. He or she must have a good eye for product quality. It is very important to check manufactured and/or expiration dates on all packaging. If the date of receipt of goods is too close to the expiration date, the officer has the authority to send them back to the supplier. A record should also be kept of what the product was and the company it came from.

D. Packaging must be inspected very closely for cracks, broken seals, the thawing and refreezing process, pest droppings, rodent urine, and so forth. This can easily be the entry point for infestation of all sorts of pests. Once these checks are made and there are traces of abuse of any sort, the entire shipment should be returned to the supplier, and a record kept of the items returned.

E.  The temperature of the goods received is also very critical. All frozen foods should be delivered in a refrigerated truck. The receiving officer should have the various thermometers to check the temperatures of the foods and verify the temperature gauge of the refrigerated truck to ensure it is below 32 degrees Fahrenheit or 0 degrees Celsius. Ensure there is no sign of thawing and refreezing.

F.  Chilled foods like dairy (milk, yogurt, cheese, etc.) should all be delivered in a refrigerated chiller truck at the right temperature, 40 degrees Fahrenheit (4.44 degrees Celsius) or below, but not freezing, as this can damage the quality of certain foods. Make the checks outlined above.

G. It's a good practice to visit your suppliers' manufacturing plant and warehouses to see and learn about how and what they do to get the best quality products and produce delivered to your property. If a supplier does not want you to do a visit and a walk-through of his or her establishment, that should be a red flag, and you should seek another supplier who has established cleaning and sanitation standards in place.

H. It is always a best practice to purchase foods from reputable and certified food suppliers. Don't put your guests and establishment at risk for food poisoning and lawsuits just to save a few dollars. You might end up having to shell out millions and harm your reputation. Can you put a value to that, and is it worth it?

Storage

After receiving all the products and produce of the highest quality, based on your intelligent level of selection, you are well on your way to great customer satisfaction. All those working in the purchasing and receiving area should be happy. It all starts with who you select for the chef, cooks, or food-processing personnel.

The other major step is storage. One must have proper storage facilities for all types of foods. Dry storage is essential and must always be clean and sanitary for receiving foods like liquor, canned goods, sugar, flour, pastas, teas, coffee, and so forth. It is also very important that foods are stored in a specific order.

First in, first out (FIFO) is the established way of managing the food movement in and out of dry storage. It greatly assists in ensuring that all foods stays fresh and are used before the expiration date. And it also assists in organization. For stacking, the fresh stock should always go to the back or bottom of the same type of product. Labeling and/or dating stock is another way to ensure stock count and proper stock rotation is achieved.

Foods should also be stored by food types. Juices, canned fruit, canned meat, spices, and pastas should all have individual designated areas.

Bulk items should also be properly separated and then resealed for long storage. Large food-grade storage containers can be purchased for those purposes.

Pay close attention in your storage areas to the same things you policed in the receiving process. You must follow through in the storage area, keeping your eyes out for pests, droppings, and nibbles on boxes, shelves, and packaging. Any item with a broken package should be disposed of, and all sealed food must be washed and sanitized. A pest control company must treat the entire storage area. It is essential that the proper PPE is worn in the disposal process. Some products may provide information for proper disposal, so please follow those instructions for your safety and that of the environment.

Sanitation

$\mathcal{S}$anitation is not the only step to producing safe food. However, in an institutional environment, it is the most important. In a restaurant or a hotel, many people from various walks of life will be staying or dining. Neither you nor your staff has any idea about who has the common cold, flu virus, hepatitis, HIV, or gastroenteritis, so sanitation in the institutional environment is essential.

The layout of the plant, type of equipment used, water quality, and pest control program all play a part in the delivery of safe food to customers. Proper cleaning and sanitation procedures are paramount to the success of your food-service operation.

When we clean and then sanitize properly, there are many benefits, including removing soils and dirt, eliminating most microorganisms, extending life of all foods, enhancing food safety, preventing cross-contamination, eliminating bad odors, providing good dining experiences, and reducing risk of lawsuits.

There are simple yet very effective ways of maintaining a good sanitation program to keep your operation running smoothly while protecting your investment. Everything must be done to ensure the customer's expectations are met and food-safety standards are adequately maintained. In the food business, it is very easy to lose a customer because of improper sanitation practices.

Cleaning removes the visible soils and particles, and sanitizing kills the bacteria and other microorganisms on the surface that can cause food-borne illnesses. Wash, rinse, and sanitize all food-preparation areas after each use to prevent cross-contamination. All kitchen and food-preparation areas must have a three-compartment sink in order to follow established cleaning and sanitation procedures.

The three compartments are for washing to remove all soils, rinsing the soils and detergent from the utensils, and sanitizing utensils that will kill the bacteria on the surface. The main reason many establishments do not adhere to the third step is because, while we can see a difference after the wash and rinse steps, we cannot see the results of sanitation with our naked eye. However, this step is very important in preventing your establishment from being exposed to the risk of outbreaks.

If a food-borne illness is traced back to your operation, you could face some very serious consequences, such as negative publicity and lawsuits. Compensation for affected customers can run from thousands to millions of dollars. It's very important to have insurance to assist or cover these expenses; otherwise the expenditure could be large enough to force you out of business.

It should be noted that sanitizing does not kill all pathogens. Most sanitizers kill 99.999 percent of all microorganisms in a square centimeter so some microorganisms still may be present on the surface under the right food, acidity, time, temperature, oxygen, moisture (FATTOM) conditions. These microorganisms can multiply at a rate of 100 percent every twenty minutes.

Not complying with proper established cleaning and sanitation procedures can result in a biofilm, a micro colony of bacteria attached to inert surfaces. Once in place, the biofilm provides a suitable environment for the bacteria, protecting them from sanitizers, cleaners, temperatures, and pH. Once a biofilm is in place, it is extremely difficult to remove. The best defense against a biofilm formation is regular and complete cleaning and sanitation of all food-preparation surfaces and equipment.

Using color-coded cutting boards helps prevent cross-contamination in food establishments and assists your sanitation program significantly. Colors assigned for each type of food may vary, but the important thing is that staff is trained in using the same color-coded cutting board for the same food type.

Below is an example of a color-coded chart.

Color	Food
Red	Raw meat
Green	Fruits and vegetables
Yellow	Raw poultry
Blue	Raw fish and seafood
Brown	Cooked meats
White	Baked goods
Purple	Allergen-free foods

Remember that chicken may have Campylobacter jejuni and salmonella, and beef may have E. coli. You don't want to use the beef cutting board for chicken, or vice versa, as this can result in cross-contamination. If this occurs, very strict cleaning and sanitation procedures must be adhered to in order to kill bacteria on the cutting boards to prevent further contamination. Cutting boards must be washed, rinsed, and sanitized after each use.

Sanitation stations should be installed throughout the kitchen and at all key points in the flow of food preparation for persons to clean and sanitize their preparation areas as they work. This reduces the risk of cross-contamination and the spread of food-borne illnesses. Procedural cleaning and sanitation wall charts must be in place as silent trainers in food-safety guidelines to keep sanitation at the forefront of all food-service employees' minds.

Your chemical supplier can do training in cleaning and sanitation for the products used in the operation. The suppliers will also provide wall charts.

Temperature

$$O^2$$

$\mathscr{P}$roper temperature control is another very important aspect of food safety. To keep it simple, to maintain the safety of food for consumption, hot foods must be kept hot, and cold foods must be kept cold. Remember the TDZ is ideal for bacteria growth and reproduction, and proper established cleaning and sanitation procedures must therefore be observed.

Temperatures should be checked with a metal stem thermometer. The instrument must be calibrated to deliver the correct temperatures. Fill a clean pail with crushed ice and water, and immerse the thermometer in the liquid for one minute. The reading should be 0 degrees Celsius or 32 degrees Fahrenheit. If this is not achieved, the thermometer must be calibrated.

All cooked foods must reach a specific internal temperature in order to kill bacteria and make the food safe for consumption. Cook all foods to the correct temperature:

- Fish, beef, and pork: 63 degrees Celsius or 145 degrees Fahrenheit
- Ground beef and injected meat: 68 degrees Celsius or 155 degrees Fahrenheit
- Poultry and wild game: 74 degrees Celsius or 165 degrees Fahrenheit
- Beef roasts: 63 degrees Celsius or 145 degrees Fahrenheit for three minutes / 55 degrees Celsius or 130 degrees Fahrenheit for twelve minutes

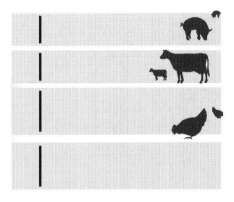

For a stuffed product, reheat and cook stuffing separately. Then stuff already cooked meat.

To shorten reheating time, reheat in small batches for proper heat transfer. Heat all foods to 74 degrees Celsius or 165 degrees Fahrenheit for a minimum of twenty seconds. Remember to discard food if it is not consumed and cannot be reheated within two hours. After cooking, keep all hot food out of the TDZ.

The use of proper equipment, such as steamers, warmers, and hot boxes to maintain correct temperatures, is essential in keeping food safe for consumption.

Refrigeration

Two basic processes can be accomplished in refrigeration: cooling and freezing.

Cooling

This is done by bringing the temperature down to below 5 degrees Celsius or 40 degrees Fahrenheit. This removes the food from the TDZ, hence prolonging the life of the food. Maintaining proper cooling temperatures can preserve the life of the food, depending on the food type, for many days. It is very important that all foods in the refrigerator are properly sealed to maintain moisture levels, to prevent cross-contamination, and to prevent circulatory air in the cooler space from depositing any airborne bacteria onto the food. Avoiding spillage and malodor are other good reasons for sealing foods. Cooling will also slow the growth of bacterial growth that may be present on the food because of improper handling procedures. Foods will eventually spoil if not consumed by the expiration date on packaging. Foods like milk, yogurt, eggs, and cheeses must be refrigerated in order to remain safe for consumption.

When cooling hot foods for refrigeration, it is very important to bring the food out of the TDZ very quickly. A blast chiller and ice bath are good methods of cooling foods quickly and safely. It is also helpful to cool foods in smaller portions based on order expectations and stir foods while they are cooling to reduce cooling time.

Freezing

This process in refrigeration takes place at 32 degrees Fahrenheit or 0 degrees Celsius and below. Freezing is very important for long-term storage, but the foods cannot be stored forever. Freezing prolongs the life of foods and meats until they are ready for usage. It is very important to track all refrigeration temperatures on a daily basis to ensure proper temperatures are being maintained so food, meats, and vegetables will not spoil.

Because freezers use large amounts of electricity, it is very important to ensure all door seals are in good condition and the system is serviced every three months for maximum efficiency. Failure to service the equipment can result in higher energy costs and spoilage. A reputable refrigeration company should do this. When receiving refrigerated products:

- Put refrigerated and frozen products in the proper storage areas immediately. Don't leave them in the receiving area in the TDZ.
- Always receive all cold foods at the correct temperatures, 5 degrees Celsius or 40 degrees Fahrenheit (refrigerated) and 0 degrees Celsius or 32 degrees Fahrenheit (frozen).
- Recognize that a dirty receiving area can present a risk to food safety.
- Inspect all goods carefully. Look for damaged packaging, as this can be the first stage of infestation on your property.
- Check for swollen or dented cans, as this has the potential to cause food poisoning that can be deadly.
- Do not accept products close to or past the expiration date.
- Purchase all foods from reputable suppliers.

Sanitizing

Two methods—heat and chemicals—can achieve sanitation. Both processes are used in various applications to kill bacteria, and each is best suited to particular applications.

Heat Sanitizing

Heat is widely used to sanitize dish machines, kitchen utensils, pots and pans, and so forth. Time plays an important role in killing microorganisms. Sanitizing may be reached by immersing utensils in a body of water between 175 and 185 degrees Fahrenheit for a minimum of one to five minutes. There is also a chemical equivalent to the high temperature.

Hot water for sanitizing is easy to apply and kills a broad spectrum of microorganisms. It is readily available from the broiler or electric booster. You must wear your PPE, as hot water can be a serious hazard and cause severe burns to the user and anyone nearby. The downside of these heating systems is that it can be quite costly to get the water heated, depending on the temperature differential, size, and flow rate of the system. Hot-water sanitizing may also contribute to biofilm formation and can damage sensitive materials like seals and gaskets. Spores may be able to survive the temperature of the water as well.

Hot-water sanitizing of large equipment is usually not recommended. The water temperature may change as some surfaces may be below the required temperature for sanitizing. This form of disinfection is only appropriate when the correct temperature can be maintained.

Chemical Sanitizing

Chemicals are used daily in food-production plants, restaurants, and food-preparation areas worldwide. This is the modern way of sanitizing to kill microorganisms. Many different types of sanitizers are used to kill various pathogens. The main sanitizers used in food areas are chlorine, quaternary, and iodophors.

Each type of sanitizer has its specific range for killing microorganisms. Chlorine and quaternary sanitizer are most widely used because of their effectiveness and price. Sanitizer kills 99.999 percent of all microorganisms but not necessarily all spores. Several factors affect effectiveness, including the water quality (hardness and micros), the surface contact exposure time, the pH of the solution, the cleanliness of the surface being sanitized (as soils use up sanitizer), and the use of the correct concentration each and every time.

Chlorine Sanitizer

Chlorine is the most commonly used sanitizer in many parts of the world for food-production plants and food-preparation areas. It is very effective at the right concentration and time exposure and, in most cases, is also very cost effective. Again, the effectiveness depends on some important conditions—for example, water quality. Iron, manganese, and ammonia in the water use up the chlorine. Too little chlorine concentration is ineffective; too much is extremely dangerous to the food and the equipment. It also leaves a strong smell that does not compliment foods.

In water over 145 degrees Fahrenheit, the chlorine will start to gas, and little or no sanitation will take place. The contact exposure time is also a factor. A minimum of one minute is required.

The residual chemical and impurities in the water use up some of the chlorine; the rest is called free chlorine, which is left to do the job of killing the microorganisms. Test kits are available from reputable chemical suppliers that can be used to check for free chlorine. Your chemical supplier can also ensure you have adequate free chlorine. Your supplier can do the water hardness checks.

Chlorine, in its liquid state, is relatively unstable, and its concentration must therefore be checked frequently. Chlorine will lose some of its ability to sanitize, as it can lose its potency naturally.

Sunlight and time are two factors that can decrease the chlorine concentration. Sanitizer concentration for food-preparations areas and equipment should be between 100–200 ppm of free chlorine for one minute. This is equivalent to the proper temperature of hot-water sanitizing. There is no need for rinsing at this concentration. For other areas like walls, floors, and so forth, 800–1000 ppm is the standard. Pay close attention to soft metals. Rinsing is very important at this concentration.

Operators can heavily overuse chlorine, so it is very important to have a control system in place, along with a dispenser set at the required concentration to meet the required sanitizing standard. High concentrations of chlorine can cause damage to equipment, leaving tiny holes in stainless steel in which microorganisms can live and thrive. It is also very corrosive and can destroy surfaces. A high concentration can also kill good bacteria and enzymes in the sewage treatment system.

It is important to wear PPE, including eyewear, when using chlorine. Handle chorine with care and avoid spills. Ensure the area is well ventilated to avoid inhaling the chlorine gas.

Please see the formula that can be used to calculate the correct amount of chlorine to add to potable water or a body of water to achieve the desired concentration. It is important to bear in mind that various concentrations of chlorine are available.

Sample Calculation

In an example, 250 liters of 200 ppm chlorine solution is required. Unscented household bleach is available as chlorine source (5.25 percent chlorine). The formula is as follows:

$$\frac{(\text{Desired ppm of chlorine}) \times (\text{total water volume})}{(\% \text{ hypochlorite in sanitizer}) \times (10{,}000)} = \text{liters concentrated chlorine to add}$$

So, using the example above:

$$\frac{(200 \text{ ppm chlorine}) \times (250 \text{ liters})}{(5.25\%) \times (10{,}000)} = 0.95 \text{ liters required}$$

Quaternary Sanitizer

Quaternary ammonium compounds, or quats, are used in similar circumstances as chlorine, but they are much safer on the food-preparation area and equipment. Quats have residual killing activity because they adhere to surfaces. They are also good for cleaning walls, floors, and drains. A good concentration for quats is 200–400 ppm. Quats have an excellent wide spectrum, killing the ability of the film-forming residual. They have low toxicity, are simple to use, and have a good shelf life.

Unlike chlorine, quats are noncorrosive, odorless, and nonstaining. Quats will not change the taste or odor of foods. It is the choice disinfectant for most hospitals and health institutions. The product is stable. Under normal conditions of storage and use, hazardous polymerization will not occur.

Quats work well in a wide pH range and are effective at killing yeast, mold, E. coli, and salmonella. However, hard water can diminish their effectiveness. Quats without surfactants at 200–400 ppm is free rinsing. The residual kill is up to approximately twenty-four hours.

Iodophor Sanitizer

Iodophor sanitizers have been around for a long time. Their base is iodine, a very powerful and helpful sanitizer and disinfectant used in World War II to fight many diseases and save many lives through its excellent sanitizing capabilities. This type of sanitizer is used for pots and pans, floors, walls, food-preparation areas, and food-production plants. When its strength is becoming weak, the iodine color (reddish brown) returns to the natural color of water. The disadvantage is that iodine stains some materials, such as plastics.

The concentration for iodophor sanitizers is 12.5–25 ppm. The utensils being sanitized should be completely submerged in the solution for one minute. Allow utensils to air-dry. At this concentration, utensils require no rinsing.

Iodophors are used in hospitals as disinfectants against a broad spectrum of microorganisms.

Chemical Products for Cleaning and Sanitizing

To keep operations clean and sanitary, it is vital that you have a good line of cleaning and sanitizing products that meet local and international standards. The US Environmental Protection Agency (EPA) and Occupational Safety and Health Administration (OSHA) play a very important role in this area.

Products that are tried and tested are best to keep your establishment clean, sanitary, and environmentally friendly. These products are designed for proper handwashing, sanitizing between handwashes, and degreasing of carbon buildup on stoves and grills. They are also powerful floor cleaners to remove heavy soil, germs, grease, and so forth. Sanitizers that will kill a broad spectrum of bacteria include stainless-steel polishes, enzyme presoaks for flatware, enzymatic grease-management products, powerful detergents, and rinse additives for dish machines, glass washers, and manual pots and pans washers.

With all these products, you will need dispensers to control the release of products where applicable. Wall charts must also be made available to give directions on the proper use and guidelines about the products. Your chemical supplier will provide the necessary material to complete the program recommended for your operation.

Apart from the provider-supplied product, it is absolutely important that MSDS are provided for each chemical product in the operation. These serve very important purposes, particularly when there is an accident such as a spillage that comes into contact with the eye or skin. The MSDS is very important for medical emergency situations, as a doctor or nurse can zoom in more accurately on the cause of the problem and could save a person's life.

Material safety data stations (right-to-know station) should be set up at various locations in the operation. All MSDS must be lodged in the right-to-know station.

Below is a table of the products needed in a cleaning and sanitizing program. (These are only averages, as product dilution can change from various suppliers. Soil classification will also determine dilution.)

Product Guide Chart

Products	Purpose	Avg. Dilution	ppm/temp	Exposure time
Antibacterial hand soap	Handwashing	2 milliliters/ wash	N/A Warm water	20 seconds
Sanitizer	Kill bacteria	Quats 200–400 ppm	80 degrees Fahrenheit	1 minute

Sanitizer	Kill bacteria	Chlorine	50–100 ppm	1 minute
Sanitizer	Kill bacteria	Iodine	12.5–25 ppm	
Heavy-duty degreaser	Remove carbon and grease	Ready to use	Full strength 120 degrees Fahrenheit	5–10 minutes
Floor cleaner	Remove soil	2 ounces per gal average	N/A 120 degrees Fahrenheit	2 minutes
Pot and pan detergent	Clean pots and pans	1–2 ounces per gal average N/A	80 degrees Fahrenheit	2 minutes
Machine detergent	Plates and glasses	5 milliliters per gal	20 ppm 150 degrees Fahrenheit	1 minutes
Machine rinse	Plates and glasses	1 milliliter per rack	N/A 180 degrees Fahrenheit	30 seconds
Machine descaler	Remove calcium	1 gallon–12 gallons water	N/A 150 degrees Fahrenheit	10–20 minutes
Grease trap cleaner	Digest grease	Ready to use	5–20 ounces N/A	nightly
Oxygen bleach	Remove tea and coffee	50–100 ppm	170 degrees Fahrenheit	1–2 minutes

The Butcher Shop

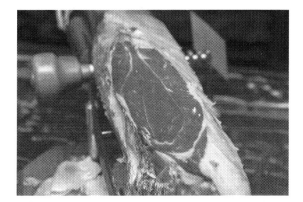

This is a highly sensitive area, and extreme care and attention must be carried out here to maintain established cleaning and sanitation procedures. There are many reasons why we must take great care of this vulnerable area. There are various types of meats in butcher shops, such as chicken, pork, beef, lamb, and fish.

These various meats all carry different types of bacteria. Bacteria buildup is a common and very serious problem. All countertops, chopping blocks, saws, slicers, and so forth, must be cleaned and sanitized after every use; when changing from one meat to another; and every three to four hours. This must be done to prevent the growth and spread of harmful bacteria.

A sanitizing station should always be in place in the butcher shop, which should be fully tiled to allow proper daily cleaning and sanitizing of all walls and equipment. Guide charts should always be in place to outline all the necessary steps to sanitize this area. Failure to follow these steps will cause malodor and the growth of many different strains of bacteria.

There are several types of bacteria that can be found in meats.

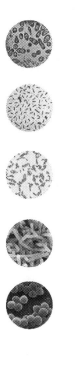

Racking

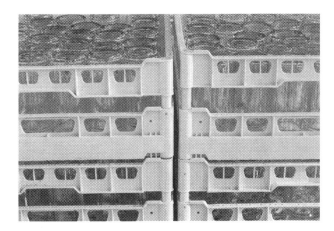

*W*ith dish machines and glass washers in your establishment to assist with your cleaning and sanitizing, you will need various types of racks for dishes and glasses, as racks play a very important role in reduced breakage, excessive handling, cross-contamination, and accidents and improved sanitation.

The various plates and glasses will have to be measured to acquire the correct length and width to size the rack appropriately. The code and brand of the glasses can also give the specific rack needed from reputable suppliers. An undersized rack will cause breakage, and there is a huge cost involved in this, as glass replacement can run into thousands of dollars. Racks that are too large prevent proper handling as the glasses will be too deep in the rack compartment.

The entire dining room setup should have enough racks for glasses. The back of the house holds 50 percent to use for storage and rotation. These racks are used in the dish machines and glass washers to wash, rinse, and sanitize all plates and glassware. Flatware racks are designed to handle all flatware in the dishwasher.

All racks must sit on a rack dolly, which must be a minimum of six inches off the floor for transportation to the dining hall and storage when not in use. Racks can be color-coded and branded with the name of the glass for easy identification. Storage areas can also have designated areas for the various types of glassware. Each glass rack should only have the specific type of glass in the compartments. This allows proper stacking, simplified taking of stock, easy dining room setup, the reduction of breakage, and increased savings.

Plates can also be placed securely in dish dollies right after the dishwashing process. Dollies can have a capacity of two hundred to four hundred plates, depending on the size of the plate. Just like the glass dollies, plate dollies can be wheeled into the dining area for setup. Right, the various dollies can be wheeled safely back to the dish room for storage. With this procedure there will certainly be a great decrease in breakage, accidents, and handling, reducing cost and improving sanitation.

There is also an effective flatware system. On your soil-side dish table, you can set up three flatware racks: one for forks, another for spoons, and the other for knives. For the dish machine they are first washed in a flatware rack (open rack). The second will be loaded in the respective flatware baskets with the eating ends up and then sent into the dish machines to be washed, rinsed, and sanitized. The flatware can hold food scraps very easily, and soils can be trapped between flatware as well, hence the need for the double washes. The wash temperature in a high-temperature machine is 150 degrees Fahrenheit (65.56 degrees Celsius) to remove grease, starches, and protein soils. The final rinse temperature is 180 degrees Fahrenheit (82.22 degrees Celsius). That temperature kills all bacteria present on the wares, and along with the rinse additive, it aids in the quick drying of the wares. All wares should dry in one minute.

From there, all wares go into their various racks for storage with very little handling. Dolly covers are available to contain all items safely during the storage period.

Pest Control

Pests continue to be a huge problem in the food-safety industry. Measures must be taken to prevent the infestation of any type of pest. The main headaches are cockroaches, rats, mice, flies, and ants. Once pests have invaded your property, it is very difficult to get rid of them. They carry many diseases, and it is very important to take the necessary steps to ensure they do not come in contact with food.

The purchasing department and receiving area personnel have very important roles to play in preventing infestation. Many different types of foods are ordered and received at the property daily, and you must be extremely careful when items arrive that they are not carrying pests or their eggs, droppings, or toxins. Thorough examination must take place at this point to ensure that no type of infestation gets into the storeroom, which can then move to other sensitive areas in the food-preparation areas and additional parts of the property.

The manner in which garbage and waste is handled, particularly in the food-and-beverage department, is crucial in the control or elimination of various pests. Food containers must be discarded of properly. Waste receptacles should always have covers to prevent rats, ants, flies and roaches, and so forth, from entering the waste bins. Food and water is the key to their survival so not a scrap of food must be left lying around anywhere for them to feed on. When garbage bins are damaged, it's very important to replace them.

Pests like to live in dark areas, cracks in the wall, and ceilings. We do not visit or pay attention to these areas on a daily basis. Pests will take food back to these areas for later use and for their young to feed and grow. These homes are out of sight, and it will take a specialist to address these problem areas for you. Two of the most important relationships to have when you have an infestation problem are with the health inspector and a reputable pest control company. The visit from the pest control company must be far more frequent than that of the health inspector, and the extent of the problem determines the number of visits. It is recommended that the pest company does its service at night when there is little or no activity in the areas being treated. The trained personnel know exactly what to do to help rid your operation of pests. A report should be done on all the areas that were treated, and the next scheduled visit should be set. Your chief steward or supervisor should be taking care of that situation.

A good cleaning-and-sanitation program is essential for the prevention or elimination of pests. Without it, infestation will continue. Know the signs of pest activity, and report observation of any such activity to the manager. Seal all openings to prevent pests from entering the building. Automatic door closure is helpful in keeping doors closed. Use fly systems to capture flies that may enter the area. Clean and sanitize all areas properly day and night to make it difficult for pests to find food.

Having a good pest control program in place is a good start. However, spraying alone will not solve the problem. Establishing a contract with a certified pest control operator is the best option when you have a pest problem. It would be even better to have this contract in place before a problem arises. You must work with your pest controller to help develop a two-way plan for pest management.

The pest controller should start with a thorough inspection of the property, inside and outside. The controller will use chemicals like commercial insecticides, bait and bait stations, and traps to eliminate the pests. Make sure you collect your updated records from the pest controller. There should be set times for the pest controller to visit the property, carry out the checks, reset all stations, and spray the various areas for treatment. These are areas only for the controller.

You can observe the property in his or her absence to ensure that important areas are not being further infested. Check packaging for reentry of more pests from the suppliers.

Solid Waste Management

*F*ood-service providers must have a good waste management program. The EPA recommends three important steps for managing waste:[7]

1. Reduce the amount of waste produced. Where possible, buy items that are concentrated, and dilute as you need. Purchase items in biodegradable packaging. Packaging that is compactable or stackable all assist greatly in reduction of waste.
2. Reuse. Provided that containers are food-safe, they can be reused after being washed, rinsed, and sanitized.
3. Recycle. You can set up a recycling program for various materials. Generally, paper, plastic, glass, and oil are part of a typical recycling program. It is a great part of a sustainable program. A recycling company or other companies usually collect the items in the recycle program to be reused for various manufacturing purposes.

The more you reduce, reuse, and recycle, the less waste that makes it into the landfill, and the less costs required for trucking. These steps are good environmental practices.

---

[7] https://www.epa.gov/recycle.

The Health Inspector

*W*hen the health inspector visits the property, he or she will be looking for food-safety compliance, such as correct high and low temperatures, and proper cleaning and sanitation procedures, if he or she is very knowledgeable and experienced. Remember the health inspector has the immediate, on-the-spot authority to shut down the operation if it is not compliant with the health standards set out in local laws. This is applicable not only to pest control but to the cleaning and sanitation of the entire property.

The health inspector will pay close attention to signs of pest infestation. This can come in several forms.

Major Areas of Infestation

- Rat infestation: all types of rats and mice, rat droppings, urine, and smell
- Roaches: all types of roaches, their eggs, droppings, and dead roaches
- Ants: all types and their trails.
- Flies: all types, mainly fruit flies and houseflies, which love garbage and will take toxins back to clean food areas, causing contamination

The health inspector will also look at the process of how garbage is handled and disposed of and how containers are being stored at the property to prevent the breeding of mosquitoes in stagnant water.

In the Food Areas

The health inspector will check temperatures, including the wash and rinse temperature of the dish machine. If it is a low-temperature unit, the sanitizer strength required will be in ppm. A chlorine-type sanitizer can be used. The freezers and chillers will also be checked to ensure they are within the safe temperature range. Checks will also be made on the inside of the units for proper storage, labeling, and packaging.

Hot foods must be kept hot, and that is out of the TDZ. This will prevent the growth of bacteria. Your inspector may use a thermometer (digital is best) to check the temperatures of the various foods on display for consumption. Cold foods are very much the same. They must also be out of the TDZ.

The floors will be inspected for soils and grease film that can cause many accidents. Cracked floor tiles and water settlement in cracks can carry serious penalties. Remember—antislip floors/tiles are the best for the food-preparation areas.

The exhaust fan(s) must be drafting the air in the right direction and out of the area. Grease will build up in the hood and filters, which can be a safety and health hazard. Your inspector will shut down the business for this reason and demand the hood and filters be property cleaned and a cleaning program implemented. Grease fires are very dangerous to the staff and the building. The exhaust system must have a fire suppression system in the event there is a fire.

Grease and oil drafted by the exhaust fan into the roof can cause leaks and deterioration, which requires expensive repair and makes work areas slippery and unsafe. Roof fires are especially hazardous. A single spark can cause a fire in a roof heavily coated with grease and oil. This type of fire is very difficult to control, and it is quite possible that you will lose your roof or the entire property. It is therefore very important that a good, preventative exhaust hood and grease-management program is in place to prevent a potentially catastrophic event. As the old saying goes, "Don't be penny wise and pound foolish."

Employee Procedures

*T*he stewarding department is generally responsible for cleaning and sanitation at restaurants, hotels, cruise ships, and food-production facilities. The executive stewarding manager is the key person responsible for cleaning and sanitation. This is a very serious area of responsibility, and everyone must adhere to his or her principles and policies to maintain established cleaning and sanitation practices for food safety. Smaller institutions may not have full stewarding departments but will have staff assigned to these tasks. The following information outlines the many important responsibilities of these employees.

Job Title: Steward
Department: Stewarding
Reports To: Stewarding Manager

I. Summary of Position: The major function of the steward is to carry out the assignments for cleaning and sanitation duties and any other areas management deems necessary. Although there is a breakdown of stewarding positions, all stewards are expected to work in any one of the positions when asked, with the exception of the night cleaner position. The various positions in stewarding are the following:

- General Steward(s): responsible for washing dishes and pots and general cleaning and sanitation of the kitchen(s)
- Utility Steward(s): responsible for trash removal, floor and wall cleaning, and special cleaning tasks and assisting general stewards during busy periods
- Silver Polisher(s): responsible for polishing all silverware used and assisting general stewards during busy periods and banquet requisition.
- Banquet Steward(s): responsible for storage and setting up equipment for banquets (banquet requisitions); assisting the banquet kitchen plate-ups; delivering food to the banquet location and traying food for waitstaff; cleaning and sanitizing the banquet kitchen after production and prior to service; and cleaning and sanitizing all dishes, pots, silver, and glassware associated with banquet functions
- Night Cleaner(s): responsible for travel removal and the cleaning and sanitizing of all food-and-beverage areas, including equipment dish machines, glass washers, floors, walls, ceiling vents, floor mats, and counters

II. Supervision Exercised
- Direct: None
- Indirect: None

III. Supervision Received
- Direct: Supervisor
- Indirect: Assistant Stewarding Manager

IV. Preferred Knowledge/Qualifications
- Able to communicate at all levels and follow instructions
- Good physical condition to do cleaning
- Able to lift up to seventy pounds
- Good sight and hearing
- No chemical allergies
- Must be flexible with work schedule

V. Tasks/Responsibilities
- Familiarization
  - Prepare for work
  - Become familiar with steward storage areas, steward cleaning and sanitation equipment, and chemicals used in stewarding and know MSDS
  - Check out keys
- Dish Machine Operation
  - Understand dish machine operation
  - Load and unload the dish machine
  - Delime the dish machine and service wash-and-rinse areas
- Cleaning/Sanitizing
  - Clean stove, range, hoods, fryers, air vents, walls, ceilings, floors, and delivery bay
  - Clean and sanitize counters; food-preparation areas; shelving; garbage cans; vegetable cutters and peelers; coffee, tea, and milk dispensers; glass coffeemaker; blenders; walk-in freezers; bread boxes; vegetable bins; and dry food storage
  - Clean and delime steam table
  - Understand cardboard compactor operation, recycling procedures, and the refrigerated garbage room operation
- Burnishing
  - Understand the burnishing machine
  - Presoak, detarnish, and burnish silverware
  - Presoak flatware
  - Use coffee and tea stain remover
  - Become familiar with daily polishing duties

- Banquets
  - o Understand banquet event orders (BEOs)
  - o Prepare for functions
  - o Understand silver uses
  - o Know food delivery times, the sizes of hot and cold carts, and what to bring to a plate-up
  - o Set up hot cart and the delivery soup
  - o Plate-up and deliver salads
  - o Do plate-ups
  - o Follow the banquet steward's checklist
- Night Cleaner
  - o Understand the night cleaner responsibilities
  - o Prepare for off-premise catering
- Major Responsibilities as a Staff Member
  - o Report to work on time
  - o Maintain all proper uniforms and appearance codes according to the grooming standard of the establishment
  - o Follow all position assignments given by superiors or manager
  - o Practice teamwork and communication with coworkers
  - o Take breaks only as assigned, or check first with the supervisor or manager before taking lunch or dinner break (which should be no longer than sixty minutes)
  - o Follow safety procedures and policies to ensure a safe working environment
  - o Maintain clean and sanitary work areas
  - o Attend all department meetings

Training Profile

Name: _____

Position: Supervisor

Department: Stewarding

Task   Employee / Date
                                                    Trainer / Date

1. Become familiar with all stewarding   _____ _____
    responsibilities
                                               _____ _____
2. Prepare the monthly labor forecast   _____ _____

3. Prepare schedules for the staff   _____ _____

4. Prepare the daily labor report   _____ _____

5. Prepare computerized payroll   _____ _____

6. Order the cleaning supplies   _____ _____

7. Handle department emergencies   _____ _____

8. Train employee in MSDS   _____ _____

                                               _____ _____

Stewarding Assistant Manager
Training Topics

Monthly Labor Forecast
- Base the forecast on restaurant and banquet activity
- Use the monthly occupancy forecast

Scheduling
- Base scheduling according to hotel occupancy and/or restaurant reservations
- Use the BEO
- Consider the outlet forecasts
- Schedule according to the staffing guide for stewarding

Daily Labor Report
- Total all hours from the daily sign-in sheet / swipe card
- Break down the hours according to the different shifts
- Total the hours
- Turn in the daily report before ten in the morning

Payroll
- Prepare weekly payroll
- Match the payroll total hours to the total hours from the daily labor reports
- Input hours for holidays, sick leave, compassionate leave, jury duty, and so forth
- Turn in every Thursday evening

Supply Ordering
- Use the par stock
- Take inventory
- Order only what is needed
- Do not go over budget
- Use a general storeroom requisition

Handle Department Emergencies (Examples)
- Sick calls and no-shows
- Last-minute requests—for example, requisitions
- Machine breakdowns
- Crunch times
- Accidents
- Cancellations of functions
- Inclement weather program
- Fire emergencies

Train All Staff on MSDS
- Ensure all staff are familiar with chemicals and first aid

Training Plan For:

Name: _____

Position: Steward/Stewardess

Department: Restaurant

Goal: To orient and train a newly hired, promoted, or transferred employee

By the end of training the employee will know and understand code of conduct, department policies, and department standards. The employee will be able to provide guest services and interact professionally with all personnel.

First-day orientation, tour,
training manuals given, and so forth _____ _____

New Hire Orientation	Human Resources	Date
_____	_____	_____
_____	_____	_____
_____	_____	_____
_____	_____	_____

Training Schedule

Tasks to Be Taught	Trainer	Date
_____	_____	_____
_____	_____	_____
_____	_____	_____
_____	_____	_____

_____   _____   _____

_____   _____   _____

_____   _____   _____

_____   _____   _____

_____   _____   _____

_____   _____   _____

_____   _____   _____

Training profile complete and reviewed by manager: _____

Evaluation of employee training and performance: _____

Training Evaluation

Trainer(s) evaluation of steward/stewardess progress during training:

_____

_____

_____

_____

Is any retraining needed? If so, in what area?

_____

_____

When will the retraining take place? _____

This certifies that _____ has successfully completed training as

_____

Trainer signature	**Date**	**Trainee signature**	**Date**
Department Head	**Date**	**Division Head**	**Date**
Human Resources	**Date**	**Training Manager**	**Date**

Training Profile

Name: _____

Position: Steward/Stewardess

Department: Stewarding

Task   Employee / Date
                                        Trainer / Date

Familiarization

1. Come prepared for work   _____ _____

2. Become familiar with steward storage areas _____ _____

3. Become familiar with cleaning equipment _____ _____

4. Become familiar with chemicals used in   _____ _____
   stewarding/ know MSDS

5. Check out keys   _____ _____

Dish Machine Operation

1. Understand dish machine operation   _____ _____

2. Load the dish machine   _____ _____

3. Unload the dish machine.   _____ _____

4. Delime the dish machine; service wash- _____ _____
   and-rinse areas

Cleaning

1. Clean the stove and range   _____ _____

2. Clean the floors   _____ _____

3. Clean the ovens ⎯⎯⎯⎯⎯⎯ ⎯⎯⎯⎯

4. Clean and sanitize the counters, food- ⎯⎯⎯⎯⎯⎯ ⎯⎯⎯⎯
   prep areas, and shelving

5. Clean and sanitize the vegetable cutters ⎯⎯⎯⎯⎯⎯ ⎯⎯⎯⎯
   and peelers

6. Clean and sanitize the coffee, tea, and ⎯⎯⎯⎯⎯⎯ ⎯⎯⎯⎯
   milk dispensers

7. Clean and sanitize the blenders ⎯⎯⎯⎯⎯⎯ ⎯⎯⎯⎯

8. Clean the hoods, air vents, and walls ⎯⎯⎯⎯⎯⎯ ⎯⎯⎯⎯

9. Clean the fryers ⎯⎯⎯⎯⎯⎯ ⎯⎯⎯⎯

10. Clean the walk-in freezers/coolers ⎯⎯⎯⎯⎯⎯ ⎯⎯⎯⎯

11. Clean the bread boxes, vegetable bins, ⎯⎯⎯⎯⎯⎯ ⎯⎯⎯⎯
    and dry food storage

12. Clean the glass coffeemakers ⎯⎯⎯⎯⎯⎯ ⎯⎯⎯⎯

13. Clean and delime the steam tables ⎯⎯⎯⎯⎯⎯ ⎯⎯⎯⎯

14. Clean the garbage cans ⎯⎯⎯⎯⎯⎯ ⎯⎯⎯⎯

15. Clean the delivery ⎯⎯⎯⎯⎯⎯ ⎯⎯⎯⎯

16. Understand the cardboard compactor ⎯⎯⎯⎯⎯⎯ ⎯⎯⎯⎯
    operation

17. Understand the recycling procedures ⎯⎯⎯⎯⎯⎯ ⎯⎯⎯⎯

18. Understand the refrigerated garbage room operation   _____ _____

   _____ _____

Burnishing
1. Understand the burnishing machine   _____ _____

2. Presoak and detarnish the silverware   _____ _____

3. Presoak flatware   _____ _____

4. Burnish silver   _____ _____

5. Remove tea and coffee stains   _____ _____

6. Become familiar with the daily polishing duties/ schedules   _____ _____

   _____ _____

Banquets
1. Understand the banquet event order (BEO)   _____ _____

2. Prepare for functions   _____ _____

3. Understand silverware uses   _____ _____

4. Know the food delivery times   _____ _____

5. Know the sizes of the hot and cold carts   _____ _____

6. Set up the hot cart   _____ _____

7. Know the requirements for a plate-up   _____ _____

8. Set up and deliver the soup   _____ _____

   _____ _____

9. Plate-up and deliver the salads _____ _____

10. Prepare plate-ups _____ _____

11. Follow the banquet steward closing _____ _____
    checklist

12. Understand the responsibilities of the _____ _____
    night cleaner

13. Prepare for off-premise catering _____ _____

Standards and Procedures
Job Title: Steward/Stewardess
Department: Stewarding

Task #1: Prepare for work
Standard: Employees will arrive with uniforms and sign in at the scheduled work time.

Procedure

1. Allow adequate time to park and walk to the employee entrance.
2. Park in the staff parking lot.
3. Swipe in at the employee entrance when entering the building, using your magnetic card or punch clock.
4. Go to housekeeping and pick up clean and correct uniform from the staff laundry.
5. Go to the changing room, and change into your uniform, placing your day clothes and all personal effects in your locker.
6. Do not leave personal belongings in the staff changing rooms.
7. Return the used staff linen to the laundry department.
8. Follow the appearance and grooming guidelines as stated in the rules of the establishment.
9. Swipe in at your department.
10. Wear your name tag in the correct area at all times, as it is a part of your uniform.
11. Make sure your station is clean and sanitary to hand over to your coworker in the next shift.
12. Swipe your card in your department five minutes before the start of your shift.
13. Swipe out and in at your department when going to and returning from break.
14. Swipe out at the end of your shift.

15. Go to your locker and pick up your day clothes and personal effects.
16. Change into your day clothes in the staff changing room.
17. Leave the property within thirty minutes after swiping out of your department.
18. Act in a friendly and professional manner at all times.

Standards and Procedures
Job Title: Steward/Stewardess
Department: Stewarding

Task #2: Become familiar with steward storage areas
Standard: The manager, assistant manager, and the floor lead only will have a key to open locked storage areas.

Procedure

1. Retrieve the correct key for the storage area from either one of the following senior reporting staff on duty: manager, assistant manager, or floor supervisor.
2. Store the stewarding supplies and kitchen equipment from the relevant storage areas: the chemical storage room and F&B storage room.
3. Select the required stewarding supplies and kitchen equipment from the relevant storage areas: the chemical storage room and F&B storage room.
4. Return the key for the storage area to one of the following senior reporting staff on duty: manager, assistant manager, or floor supervisor.

Standards and Procedures
Job Title: Steward/Stewardess
Department: Stewarding

Task #3: Become familiar with the steward cleaning equipment
Standard: Employees are to notify management if equipment is worn or needs replacing and if supplies are low. Ensure that equipment is available and in good condition at all times. Report any defects to management.

Procedure

1. Mop and Bucket
   a. Collect the mop, bucket, and floor cleaner from the steward closet for that particular area.
   b. Through the chemical dilution system, add floor cleaning solution to the bucket. (A disinfectant cleaner is ideal for this purpose to kill bacteria present on the floor.)
   c. Spray the mop head with hot water, and wring dry before using for spills involving grease.
   d. Return all equipment to the steward closet once the job is completed.

Equipment must be clean and allowed to air-dry.

2. Broom and Dustpan
   a. Retrieve the broom and dustpan from the steward's closet, outlet, or main kitchen.
   b. Ensure any broken item—for example, glass, china, and loose debris—is swept up immediately. Use brooms and dustpans to avoid cuts from the broken glass instead of using cleaning cloths, box tops, and bare hands.
   c. Use straw broom to clean small areas and for getting in and around the equipment.

    d. Use larger brooms for cleaning the more open areas of the floor.

    e. Wear the necessary safety equipment for protection (PPE).

3. Cleaning Cloth

    a. Use a rag to wipe up small spills, clean, polish, and wipe out ovens after grease cutter has been applied.

    b. Obtain the cleaning cloth from the container located in the stewarding storage areas.

    c. Obtain additional cleaning cloths from the laundry.

4. Grill Bricks

    a. Locate and take out only the grill bricks from the chemical room.

    b. Use the grill bricks to clean the grill and griddle tops.

    c. Keep a grill brick and other equipment in their designated areas.

5. Grill Scrapers

    a. Use grill scrapers for scraping during deep cleaning and removal of heavy solids from the pots and pans.

    b. Distribute the scrapers to the night cleaners and pot washers, as needed.

6. Gloves

    a. Distribute the gloves to stewards, as required by management.

    b. Exchange old gloves for new gloves as needed.

    c. Wear gloves, aprons, and goggles at all times when using any type of cleaning compounds (chemical); refilling chemical containers; or degreasing high-temperature equipment, ovens, grills, and so forth.

7. Goggles

    a. Distribute the goggles to stewards, as required by management.

    b. Wear goggles at all times when refilling any type of cleaning chemicals; using a specific chemical; or degreasing oven, grills, and so forth.

8. Spray Bottles
   a. Locate and take out the spray bottles from the chemical closet in the compactor room.
   b. Use spray bottles for products of which they are labeled and intended for only.
   c. Use spray bottles when applying heavy-duty degreaser, stainless-steel polish, and all-purpose cleaners.

9. Squeegees
   a. Locate and select the squeegees in the chemical storeroom.
   b. Use the large size (twenty-four- to thirty-six-inch) squeegees for cleaning the floors.
   c. Use the smaller size squeegees (twelve inches) for cleaning the counters and windows.

10. Plastic Buckets
    a. Place the required supplies in each bucket for each night cleaner.
    b. Ensure the following items are in the plastic bucket:
       - scraper
       - grill stone
       - one spray bottle each of grease cutter plus, stainless-steel polish, and all-purpose cleaner
       - scrub pads
       - apron
       - cleaning cloth
       - gloves
       - goggles
       - one handheld squeegee

11. Floor Brush
    a. Locate the brushes in the cleaner closet.
    b. Use stiff brushes for scrubbing floors after the soap has been applied.

12. Power Spray Washer
    a. Locate the power spray washer in the equipment storeroom.
    b. Use to deep clean walk-ins and freezers, chillers, receiving dock, and other areas as necessary.

13. Liquid Vacuum
    a. Locate the liquid vacuum in the equipment storeroom.
    b. Do not use a wet hand to plug equipment into power supply.
    c. Use vacuum to remove the water after using the power spray washer when deep cleaning and cleaning up liquid spills.

Standards and Procedures
Job Title: Steward/Stewardess
Department: Stewarding

Task #4: Become familiar with chemicals used in stewarding and know MSDS
Standard: Never take chemicals for the dispensing units straight out of their shipping containers. Always use a dispenser, as this is safer and ensures the correct mixing of chemicals with water at all times. Safety is priority number one.

Procedure

Know MSDS for all chemicals used.

Chemical	Use
Machine detergent	Dish machine detergent for high-temperature dishwashing
Glass machine detergent	Glass machine detergent for low-temperature washing and bar-glass washing
Rinse additive	Drying agent for dish machine and glassware
Chlorinated/ quaternary	Sanitizer for low-temperature glass and dish machine
Lime Away	Deliming agent for glass and dish machines, coffee machines, steamers, and so forth (hard-water conditions)
Manual detergent	Manual pot-and-pan detergent and general-purpose cleaner
Oven Brite	Heavy-duty degreaser for ranges, hoods, and stoves for stoves, floors, walls, and equipment
Greasestrip Plus	Heavy-duty degreaser that quickly cuts through carbon and burnt-on soils

All-purpose cleaner	General cleaning of food-preparation surfaces, floors, walls, counters, and equipment
Stain remover	Bleaching of tea and coffee cups and cleaning of coffee urns and pots
Freezer cleaner	Special cleaning agent for refrigerators and freezers
Food-safe sanitizer	Sanitizer for food-contact surfaces and three-sink compartment
Nonfood sanitizer	Quaternary detergent and germicide in one for the use on garbage cans, compactor room and floors, butcher shop, and non-food-contact areas
Stainless-steel cleaner	Removal of soils and clean stainless steel surfaces
Stainless-steel polish	Polish for stainless steel after it has been cleaned
Antimicrobial soap	Soap for handwashing (all handwashing must be for twenty seconds up to elbows; use nailbrush to remove soils from under nails)
Flatware presoak	Presoak for silver products before cleaning and soap for pot washing
Silver polish	Polish for holloware, platters, samovar, and so forth
Copper polish	Polish for copperware, such as copper pans and copper chafing dishes

Standards and Procedures
Job Title: Steward/Stewardess
Department: Stewarding

Task #5: Check out keys

Standard: Sign out all steward keys with security/manager and return promptly at the end of the shift.

Procedure

1. Locate keys at the security/manager.
2. Stop and request the stewarding keys.
3. Sign your name and the time the key is requested on the key control log.
4. Open the closets where cleaning supplies are stored with the keys.
5. Return the keys at the end of the shift or at the end of the task and sign out.

Standards and Procedures
Job Title: Steward/Stewardess
Department: Stewarding

Task #6: Understand dish machine operation
Standard: It is important that the water is changed in the machines and the machines are rinsed out. The wash arms, rinse jets, and drain screens must be cleaned at least three times per day or as needed.

Procedure

There are various types of dish machines on the market: dump-and-fill machines; single-tank machines; multitank machines; or flight-type machines.

Before operating any machine:
1. Check the water reservoir tank to ensure there are no obstacles in the tank or blocking the pump intake screen or wash arms.
2. Check to ensure it is full of water and there is detergent and rinse additive in the dispensers. (If the machine is a low-temperature machine, there must also be a chemical sanitizer.)
3. Ensure the drain(s) are closed.
4. If the machine is not full of water, flip the toggle switch labeled "on."

The machine will then fill automatically to the right amount.

The detergent dispenser alarm will sound if the machine is out of detergent or rinse agent. To get detergent or rinse agent, obtain more product from the nearest storage closet or ask the floor supervisor for more supplies.

5. Press green to start and red to stop the machine.

Standards and Procedures
Job Title: Steward/Stewardess
Department: Stewarding

Task #7: Load the dish machine
Standard: Never prescrape the dishes or pots and pans into the garbage disposal. Flatware can be discarded, and this is very costly.

Procedure

1. Prewash all dishes before placing them in the dish machine.

The dish machine cannot scrub dishes. Only spray them with high-pressure hot water and detergent.

2. Locate the scrape-and-prewash station at the soil side or loading side of each dish machine.
3. Remove the excess food at the prewash unit in the scrap/prewash area.
4. Load the machine.
5. Locate the garbage disposal at each scrape-and-prewash station.
6. Scrape food left on dishes only.

The waitstaff drops off dishes prescraped and stacked in piles according to size.

7. Rinse and stack dishes until a pile of the same dishes has accumulated.
8. Load the dishes on the rack of the machine.
9. Load the dishes in batches of the same type to make the job of stacking easier.
10. Stack away the dishes by type.
11. Use a separate bus tub for cleaning the silverware.
12. Line the bus tub with tin foil.

13. Fill the bus tub with water and silver-soaking solution.
14. Collect and place the silverware into the bus tub containing the silver-soaking solution.
15. Run through on a flat rack. (It's best that the silver is sorted.)
16. Unload the machine and sort the silver into racks (baskets) that hold it upright.
17. Run the silver through for a second time in the baskets to ensure it is cleaned properly and so the water can sheet off more effectively and prevent spots and tarnishing.

Standards and Procedures
Job Title: Steward/Stewardess
Department: Stewarding

Task #8: Unload the dish machine

Standard: Use care when handling the china, glass, and silver so items are not chipped and cracked. Remove any chipped and cracked items from circulation.

Procedure

1. Take items off in groups when unloading the dish machine.
2. Stack them in racks on a cart or a plate or glass dolly located at the clean end of the dish machine.
3. Deliver the china and kitchen equipment to the proper places, or rack them for storage.
4. Stack dishes and glassware at the clean end of the machine.
5. Take the dishes and glassware to their location in the chefs' area or storeroom immediately.
6. Ensure the chefs/cooks are stocked up on dishes at the beginning of the shift.
7. Check the food supply line periodically to ensure if the dishes need replenishing.
8. Stock the waitstaff areas with pitchers and bread and butter plates, and replenish as required.
9. Assist the dishwashing steward when he or she is busy.

Standards and Procedures
Job Title: Steward/Stewardess
Department: Stewarding

Task #9: Delime the dish machine
Standard: Check and delime the dish machine once a week or as needed.

Procedure

This is necessary when lime scales develop on walls and surfaces in the dish machine.

1. Drain used water from the tank(s).
2. Close the drain valve and allow three-quarter tank of fresh water.
3. Add half-gallon of lime descaler.
4. Turn on the heat to reach a temperature of 150 degrees Fahrenheit (65.56 degrees Celsius) in the wash tank.
5. Run the machine for ten minutes, and check surfaces for lime removal.
6. Use a brush to assist in the removal of lime.
7. Extend the wash as necessary to remove lime buildup.
8. Check the rinse section of the machine, and use a spray bottle with lime descaler to remove residual lime.
9. Drain the machine.
10. Fill the tank with fresh water, and run the machine for five minutes to rinse and remove lime.
11. Use lime descaler to clean the exterior of the machine, and wipe off with a wet cleaning cloth.
12. Ensure the wash and rinse arms are clean and clear.
13. Drain the rinse water from the dish machine.
14. Fill the dish machine with fresh water and detergent for the next shift.

Standards and Procedures
Job Title: Steward/Stewardess
Department: Stewarding

Task #10: Clean stoves and ranges

Standard: Wear PPE at all times. Ensure the stoves and ranges are warm when cleaned, and take extra care not to extinguish the pilot light. Clean ranges nightly.

Procedure

1. Warm the stove/range to 140 degrees Fahrenheit (60 degrees Celsius) and then turn off the stove/range.
2. Use heavy-duty degreaser to remove carbon, grease, and oil from ranges.
3. Apply the solution with a trigger spray bottle labeled correctly with the heavy-duty degreaser evenly, and let it sit for ten minutes before removing.
4. Use the grill brick for the flat-type ranges and a brush to loosen carbon on stoves.
5. Use damp cloth to wipe up soils.

Take care not to extinguish the pilot light.

6. Check that the pilot lights are still lit when finished.

Standards and Procedures
Job Title: Steward/Stewardess
Department: Stewarding

Task #11: Clean the ovens

Standard: Clean the ovens each night, using a minimum amount of water to prevent damage to the oven.

Procedure

1. Clean the ovens at 120 degrees Fahrenheit (48.89 degrees Celsius).
2. Use heavy-duty degreaser in a correctly labeled trigger spray bottle to remove grease and oil.
3. Extend time if an oven is very dirty or has built-up or burnt-on food and carbon.
4. Scrub out the ovens with a minimum amount of water to prevent damage to oven parts.
5. Apply the grease-cutting solution.
6. Scrub the area.
7. Wipe down with damp cloth.
8. Turn on the oven fans, and leave the oven doors open to help dry the ovens.
9. Clean the oven racks in the pot sink.

Standards and Procedures
Job Title: Steward/Stewardess
Department: Stewarding

Task #12: Clean the fryers
Standard: Clean the fryers thoroughly upon the cook's request.

Procedure

1. Turn on the fryer for a few minutes so the grease becomes liquid.
2. Get a pot, strainer, and filter.
3. Carefully strain the grease through the filter into the pot.
4. Discard the grease if the cooks give instructions to do so.
5. Collect the grease in a bucket.
6. Dump the grease into the special grease container located in the compactor or garbage room.
7. After draining the grease:
    a. Fill the fryer with a solution of water and fryer cleaner.
    b. Turn the fryer to 200 degrees Fahrenheit (93.33 degrees Celsius) and allow the solution to boil for fifteen minutes or until clean.
    c. Scrub any stained areas with a brush or green pad.
    d. Turn off the heat and drain.
8. Add cold water to cleaning solution to prevent warping of the tank.
9. Rinse thoroughly with fresh hot water.
10. Leave the grease in the pot for the cooks to pour into the fryer.

Standards and Procedures
Job Title: Steward/Stewardess
Department: Stewarding

Task #13: Clean the hoods, air vents, walls, and ceilings
Standard: Clean hood, air vents, walls, and ceilings monthly.

Procedure

Hoods
1. Spray the hoods with a solution of degreaser and let it sit for ten minutes to penetrate soils.
2. Remove soils from the hoods using a cleaning cloth.
3. Soak the filters in a solution for degreaser for one hour.
4. Rinse in clean water.
5. Allow to air-dry.

Air Vents
1. Clean air vents with a cleaning cloth.
2. Apply the degreaser solution.
3. Spray on the degreaser for two minutes and then wipe with a cleaning cloth.

Walls and Ceilings
1. Use the scrub pads that carry broom handles and special pads for gripping to clean the walls and the ceilings.
2. Use a solution of detergent and degreaser.
3. Use two rods: one for the scrub pad and the other for wiping down the walls and the ceilings.

Standards and Procedures
Job Title: Steward/Stewardess
Department: Stewarding

Task #14: Clean and sanitize counters and food-preparation areas
Standard: Clean the counters and other food contact areas after each period of use. Clean the hoods, air vents, walls, and ceilings each week.

Procedure

Counters and Food-Preparation Areas
1. Clean the counters and other food-contact areas with an all-purpose cleaner and sanitize with a quaternary sanitizer.
2. Use a cleaning cloth to remove soils from the areas.
3. Use a scrub pad or brush for areas with stuck-on food or grit.
4. After cleaning, sanitize the area, and use a squeegee to remove excess water from the area.
5. Allow to air-dry.

Standards and Procedures
Job Title: Steward/Stewardess
Department: Stewarding

Task #15: Clean the floors
Standard: Use the Wet Floor signs when cleaning the floors. Dry wet floors as soon as possible to prevent slip-and-fall accidents.

Procedure

1. Put all items directly on the floor onto the table or move them to another area.
2. Relocate the fatigue mats while cleaning the area. (Return the fatigue mats to their original position after the floor has been cleaned and dried.)
3. Place Wet Floor signs in the area where the floor cleaning and mopping is being done.
4. Clean all floor drains before the floor is washed.
5. Scrub with soap and scrub pad.
6. Scrub all grates and screens.
7. Thoroughly sweep the entire floor.
8. Clean all the corners and under all equipment and shelving.
9. Note all heavily soiled areas to give them extra attention as you clean those areas.
10. Fill a mop bucket with cleaning solution.
11. Apply cleaning solution liberally to floor and scrub areas that are heavily soiled with a deck brush.
12. Allow the cleaning solution to sit for two minutes, but do not let it dry.
13. Pick up the cleaning solution with a mop dipped in clean, hot rinse water.
14. Replace soiled rinse water frequently.
15. Allow the floor to air-dry.

16. Use a portable washer to clean the floors at night.
17. Rinse the floor thoroughly, making sure to get in all the corners and under all the equipment.
18. Squeegee the floor after it has been rinsed, and push the water toward the floor drains.

The utility steward will sweep, mop, and remove trash during the shifts.

Standards and Procedures
Job Title: Steward/Stewardess
Department: Stewarding

Task #16: Clean and sanitize vegetable peelers
Standard: Disconnect power before servicing. Clean and sanitize after each use.

Procedure

Vegetable Chopper
1. Disassemble and wash all removable parts in a hot solution of detergent in the pot-and-pan sink.
2. Flush with water to loosen soils.
3. Rinse thoroughly with clean water.
4. Dip all parts in a sanitizing solution.
5. Wipe stationary components clean with a solution of detergent.
6. Sanitize by wiping with sanitizer solution.

Vegetable Peeler
1. Disconnect electrical power from the unit to avoid accidents.
2. Remove the lid, abrasive discs, perforated strainer, and chopper.
3. Flush with cold water, and clean the peel trap.
4. Wash all removed parts in pot-and-pan sink in a solution of detergent.
5. Wash the inside and outside surfaces of the stationary unit using the same solution and a long-handle brush.
6. Rinse all parts in clean water.
7. Sanitize all parts by rinsing in a solution of quaternary sanitizer.
8. Allow to dry.

Standards and Procedures
Job Title: Steward/Stewardess
Department: Stewarding

Task #17: Clean and sanitize tea and milk dispensers

Standard: Clean and sanitize daily. All milk dispensers and containers are highly susceptible to bacteria growth and must be kept immaculate and sanitary at all times.

Procedure

1. Thoroughly flush the empty dispenser with fresh water.
2. Dismantle and clean the faucet every time while wearing rubber gloves.
3. Scrub all parts of the dispenser thoroughly with a solution of detergent.
4. Thoroughly rinse with fresh water.
5. Sanitize with quaternary sanitizer.
6. Allow to air-dry.
7. Clean the exterior with all-purpose cleaner.

Standards and Procedures
Job Title: Steward/Stewardess
Department: Stewarding

Task #18: Clean blenders
Standard: Disconnect the power from the blender to avoid accidents. Clean and sanitize after each use.

Procedure

1. Remove the cup lid and blade assembly at the pot sink.
2. Wash in a solution of detergent.
3. Be careful when washing sharp blades.
4. Wipe clean the base of the blender using the same solution.
5. Submerge the cup, lid, and blade assembly only in a solution of sanitizer.
6. Remove carefully, and allow to air-dry.

Standards and Procedures
Job Title: Steward/Stewardess
Department: Stewarding

Task #19: Clean the walk-in freezers

Standard: Sweep and clean the walk-in freezers daily, and do a deep cleaning each month. Wear special low-temperature PPE.

Procedure

1. Remove all the foods that the chef needs for cooking.
2. Sweep the floors.
3. Wash the walls in the freezers with an antithaw freezer cleaner.
4. Mop the floors with hot water and floor-cleaning compound.
5. Clean all the shelving, including the large carts.
6. Follow the monthly cleaning schedule.

A certified refrigeration technician should check and service the cooling system to certify proper and efficient operation and freezing temperatures.

Standards and Procedures
Job Title: Steward/Stewardess
Department: Stewarding

Task #20: Clean the bread boxes, vegetable bins, and dry storage
Standard: Clean and sanitize weekly.

Procedure

1. Remove all food from the containers.
2. Brush up or vacuum all loose soils.
3. Wash the container in detergent.
4. Rinse with clean water.
5. Sanitize with quaternary sanitizer.
6. Allow to air-dry.

Standards and Procedures
Job Title: Steward/Stewardess
Department: Stewarding

Task #21: Clean the glass coffeemaker
Standard: Disconnect the power from the coffeemaker to avoid accidents. Clean and sanitize after each use and delime weekly.

Procedure

1. Flush the coffeemaker thoroughly with clean water between batches.
2. Empty all units and wash in a solution of detergent at the end of each period of use.
3. Rinse thoroughly with hot water.
4. Sanitize and air-dry
5. Return the units to the coffeemaker for the next day use.

To Delime
1. Wash the glass unit in a solution of descaler to remove any film or lime haze.
2. Rinse thoroughly in warm water.
3. Allow to air-dry.
4. Clean the coffeemaker with stainless steel cleaner.

Standards and Procedures
Job Title: Steward/Stewardess
Department: Stewarding

Task #22: Clean and delime steam tables
Standard: Clean daily and delime as necessary.

Procedure

1. Remove the food containers to the refrigerated storage as soon as serving is completed.
2. Turn off the heat, and drain all steam wells before cleaning.
3. Brush and wash all surfaces with a hot solution of detergent, including top backboard, front and sides.
4. Remove baked-on foods with a metal scraper.
5. Rinse with hot water and wipe dry.

Standards and Procedures
Job Title: Steward/Stewardess
Department: Stewarding

Task #23: Clean the delivery areas
Standard: Clean daily or as required.

Procedure

1. Sweep up and remove all loose trash boxes and so forth.
2. Use the Mikro Spray units to apply a hot solution of cleaner to the floor areas, Dumpster exterior, steps, ramps, and other surfaces.
3. Allow the cleaning solution to sit for five minutes but not to dry.
4. Scrub with a deck brush to remove grease deposits and strains. If there is malodor, use a disinfectant to disinfect the areas, as this will enhance the air quality in the area.
5. Spray and rinse thoroughly with hot water.

Standards and Procedures
Job Title: Steward/Stewardess
Department: Stewarding

Task #24: Operate the cardboard compactor
Standard: Maintain the compactor room free of trash, and clean nightly. Only qualified personnel whose job requires frequent use of the compactor will be issued keys. Never lend or give your key to any unauthorized person.

Procedure

1. Place the trash in the compactor. Ensure the items added fall below the recommended level. Do not overfill the compactor.
2. Check that the safety latch is secure.
3. Engage the key and start the machine only once.
4. Press start for compaction.
5. **NEVER** climb into the trash compactor to try to push down the garbage.
6. Add garbage until compacted material is at the site level.
7. After compacted garbage is securely wrapped, turn off the power.
8. Remove the safety latch to open the door and remove the compacted trash.
9. In case of an emergency, push the red safety button to shut down the compactor.

Standards and Procedures
Job Title: Steward/Stewardess
Department: Stewarding

Task #25: Use the recycling procedures
Standard: Know which items can be recycled and where each item goes in the recycling procedure. Ensure that recycling bins are present at all bussing areas.

Procedure

Recycling Room
1. Ensure the bins are clearly marked to show which is to be used for each type of recyclable item.
2. Do not place items into the wrong bin.
3. Do not put any cardboard in the recycle room.
4. Keep the floor areas clean and free of rubbish.

White Paper and Magazines
1. Do not place colored paper in this bin.
2. Put the white paper and magazines into a plastic bag, and stack them neatly in the correct bin.

Newspaper
1. Put newspapers into the drums.
2. Do not put magazines with glossy paper into this area.

Plastic
1. Remove the lids on all plastic bottles and jars before placing them into the bin.
2. Ensure that no metal (e.g., rims) are placed into the bin for plastics.
3. Place popcorn packaging and Styrofoam in the bin for plastics.

Aluminum
1. Bag the aluminum cans.
2. Put the bagged cans into the drums located in the area marked Aluminum.

Glass Only
1. Rinse all glass and china before placing them into the bin.
2. Place all glass and china into the bin marked Glass Only.
3. Do not place any other trash into the bin, as the load will be considered contaminated.

Cardboard Only
1. Break down and flatten the cardboard boxes.
2. Place the flattened boxes into the bins marked Cardboard Only.
3. Ensure there are two bins for cardboards.
4. Ensure no other trash is placed into the cardboard bins to contaminate the load.

Trash Compactor
1. Keep the trash compactor room neat at all times. Place any cardboard to be compacted into the compactor.
2. Stand clear of the Dumpster when raising and lowering the compactor.
3. Ensure any item left in the compactor has already been compacted before loading the compactor.
4. Ensure any items added to the compactor fall below the shelf level.
5. Ensure the shelf level can be seen when looking into the compactor.
6. Go to the blue-gray box located outside the fence at the end of the machine when the trash has been placed into the hole.
7. Push the key in the slot once only.
8. When trash bags get hung inside the bin and do not fall all the way into the hole of the trash compactor, remove the trash bags of possible obstructions, and place them so they go down the whole

way or use a piece of wood or broom handle to push down the
hole.

9. Never get into the trash compactor to try to push down items with
   your feet.

Oil (Filtered and Unfiltered)

1. Ensure all oil containers are kept to be reused for storing used oil
   from fryers and other areas.
2. Keep these containers in the air-conditioned garbage room until
   collection.

Standards and Procedures
Job Title: Steward/Stewardess
Department: Stewarding

Task #26: Understand the refrigerated garbage room operation
Standard: Clean and disinfect the garbage room after every garbage collection. Always wear PPE.

Procedure

1. Separate all garbage before going into the garbage room.
2. Store recyclable material on the side of the room marked Recycling Material in the air-conditioned section.
3. Place all fish and meat scrapped in the chiller section of the garbage room to reduce odor and bacteria growth.
4. Ensure both doors of the garbage room are securely closed to prevent pest infestation.

A time-release disinfectant and insecticide would assist greatly to prevent infestation and control malodor. Collection of garbage will be nightly or as necessary.

To Clean
1. Sweep up all scraps from the floor.
2. Use the pressure washer to flush the complete room with hot water and detergent.
3. Scrub the floor with a deck brush to remove tough soil.
4. Rinse the floor with clean water.
5. Disinfect the garbage room to kill germs and bacteria.
6. Use the squeegee to wipe the walls and the floor, and allow to dry.
7. Wash your hands with antimicrobial hand soap up to the elbows for twenty seconds and rinse.

All equipment used in the garbage areas are designated for these areas only.

Standards and Procedures
Job Title: Steward/Stewardess
Department: Stewarding

Task #27: Clean the garbage bins
Standard: Clean all garbage bins daily. Where possible, the garbage room should be air-conditioned and equipped with a pressure washer system with detergent and disinfectant.

Procedure

For automatic can washer:

1. Place the garbage can in the garbage can washer and close the door.
2. Press start and allow the wash cycle to be completed.
3. Remove that garbage can, and allow it to air-dry.
4. Place a garbage bag in the garbage can before restoring it to the area of use.

For manual washer:

1. Ensure to wear personal protective equipment (PPE).
2. Apply detergent and water and scrub with a brush.
3. Rinse the can with clean water.
4. Disinfect the can with a disinfectant or germicide to kill germs.
5. Drain and allow to air-dry before use.
6. Wash hands with an antibacterial hand soap.

Standards and Procedures
Job Title: Steward/Stewardess
Department: Stewarding

Task #28: Presoak and detarnish silverware
Standard: Clean and sanitize after each use.

Procedure

1. Place aluminum foil or rods in the bottom of the sink or pan.
2. Add enzymatic presoak to warm water.
3. Immerse silverware so they touch the foil.
4. Remove silverware when the tarnish is gone.
5. Place the silverware into the silver basket with the handles down.
6. Wash immediately in the dish machine.
7. Transfer the clean silverware to the empty silver basket after cooling with handles up for sorting.
8. Replace the foil when it is discolored.

Standards and Procedures
Job Title: Steward/Stewardess
Department: Stewarding

Task #29: Presoak flatware
Standard: Clean and sanitize after each use.

Procedure

1. Scrape or flush heavy soil from flatware as soon as possible after use.
2. Add presoak to warm water.
3. Immerse the flatware in the presoak solution until soil is loosened.
4. Remove the flatware, place in an open rack, and give one wash in the dish machine.
5. Place the flatware in the basket type with the handles down for a second wash.
6. Transfer the clean flatware to the empty basket with the handles up.
7. Allow the clean flatware to cool and dry.

Standards and Procedures
Job Title: Steward/Stewardess
Department: Stewarding

Task #30: Understand the burnishing machine
Standard: Use cold water in the burnishing machine to prevent the water pump from burning out. Wear thick gloves and goggles when using the burnishing machine.

Procedure

1. Keep the burnishing machine clean and in good condition at all times, as this is very important to the stewarding department.
2. Change the water after each day's use, and always use cold water.
3. Add the recommended amount of burnishing compound into the area of the ball bearings. (The silverware will come out tarnished if the ball bearings are tarnished.)
4. Allow the machine to run for ten to fifteen minutes.
5. Use thick gloves and goggles.
6. Read and follow the machine operating instructions.

Standards and Procedures
Job Title: Steward/Stewardess
Department: Stewarding

Task #31: Burnish silverware

Standard: Only use recommended burnishing powder in the burnishing machine. Change burnishing solution after every six or seven cycles.

Procedure

1. Assemble all silverware that needs burnishing.
2. Remove the cover, and add burnishing solution so it is just over the burnishing shot.
3. Always detarnish and clean silverware before burnishing.
4. Place the silverware in the burnishing machine, not exceeding the number of pieces recommended.
5. Replace the cover and start.
6. Run for five to ten minutes or longer if necessary.
7. Remove the silverware.
8. Rinse and run the silverware immediately through the dish machine.
9. Allow to air-dry.
10. Wrap the silver in plastic (cling wrap) for storage.

Standards and Procedures
Job Title: Steward/Stewardess
Department: Stewarding

Task #32: Understand silverware uses

Standard: Be able to name all silverware used. Use the proper silverware with each food item.

Procedure

1. Know what silverware goes with which food items.
2. Prepare a banquet sheet to assist in a correct setup for the silverware.
3. Ensure the proper silverware is placed as follows:
   - Soup: rounded soupspoon (bouillon spoon)
   - Butter: bread and butter (B&B) knife
   - Salad: salad fork and salad knife
   - Entrée: dinner fork and dinner knife
   - Cake for dessert: salad fork and dessert spoon

Standards and Procedures
Job Title: Steward/Stewardess
Department: Stewarding

Task #33: Understand coffee and tea stain removers and silver cream
Standard: Wear thick gloves and goggles when using silver-polishing products.

Procedure

Tea Stain Removal
1. Remove coffee and tea stains from the coffeepots, teapots, and samovars by using oxygen or chlorine stain remover.
2. Dissolve half-cup of tea stain remover in hot water.
3. Pour the solution into the coffeepot, teapot, or samovar.
4. Leave the coffeepot, teapot, or samovar to soak in the solution for ten minutes.
5. Pour out the solution and rinse the pot thoroughly.

Silver Cream
1. Wipe on silver cream with a damp sponge.
2. Polish the silverware with a clean, dry rag.
3. Rinse off the silver cream immediately.
4. Run the silverware through the dish machine.
5. Allow to air-dry.

Standards and Procedures
Job Title: Steward/Stewardess
Department: Stewarding

Task #34: Become familiar with the daily polishing duties

Standard: Polish all silverware when scheduled. Ensure all silverware in the silver room is polished at all times and wrapped in clear plastic wrap.

Procedure

1. Check and pick up all holloware and flatware that needs polishing and burnishing from the silver room every morning.
2. Polish the silverware according to the polishing schedule posted on the wall by the silver room.
3. Replace all the brass chafing dishes after breakfast breakdown daily.
4. Pick up damaged silver from the restaurant and other food-and-beverage outlets.

Standards and Procedures
Job Title: Steward/Stewardess
Department: Stewarding

Task #35: Understand banquet event orders (BEOs)
Standard: Follow the BEO carefully to ensure timely delivery of requested items. Ensure banquet stewards have BEOs and understand them.

Procedure

1. Prepare for the function by using the necessary information provided on the function sheet or BEO.
2. Check the function sheet for the following details:
   a. name of the function sheet
   b. name of the function to be held
   c. times the function will start and end
   d. detailed menu list
   e. amount of people for function
   f. type of function service—for example, plated service, buffet, French service, VIP function, VIP coffee service, and so forth
3. Use this information from the function sheet or BEO to
   a. prepare to pull china, glassware, silver, carts, and so forth;
   b. prepare the setups; and
   c. know the timing to deliver the food items.

Standards and Procedures
Job Title: Steward/Stewardess
Department: Stewarding

Task #36: Prepare for functions
Standard: Set up functions exactly and according to the BEO with no variations unless authorized to do so.

Procedure

1. Review the banquet order carefully.
2. Estimate how much china, glassware, and silverware will be used.
3. Ensure there is enough china, glassware, and silverware on hand.
4. Visit the area where the function will take place with the captain or manager, and ask questions about anything you are not sure of.
5. Discuss the BEO with the cooks, and decide what sizes of hot carts are suitable.
6. Check to ensure that all the equipment is in good working condition.
7. Ensure the units are clean, there are enough serving utensils, and the heating elements are working.
8. Obtain the china, glassware, and silverware requisitions from the banquet coordinator.
9. Prepare the buffet tables for dish-up and the breakdown stations for stewarding provided by the banquets division.
10. Assist in the dish-up.
11. Ensure the service area is kept clean and organized throughout the event.
12. Ensure all dirty dishes are returned to the kitchen and the dirty glasses are stacked on the racks.

13. Walk through the entire area to ensure all the hotel equipment has been collected.
14. Clean and sanitize all the equipment.
15. Report any broken or missing items or equipment.

Standards and Procedures
Job Title: Steward/Stewardess
Department: Stewarding

Task #37: Know food delivery times
Standard: Deliver all foods for a function exactly at the specified time.

Procedure

1. Check with the banquet chef for details of the function.
2. Ensure all buffet functions with food are ready twenty minutes before the scheduled start time.
3. Arrange and prepare plated meals.
4. Ensure all cold food is prepared twenty minutes prior to the start of the function.
5. Ensure a cold-food breakfast is delivered twenty minutes prior and placed in the banquet kitchen.
6. Ensure all buffet functions with hot food are delivered twenty minutes prior.
7. Ensure ice carvings are delivered twenty minutes prior to the start of the function for the chef and banquet steward to place in the room.
8. Ensure wedding cakes are delivered twenty minutes prior to the start of the event.

Standards and Procedures
Job Title: Steward/Stewardess
Department: Stewarding

Task #38: Know the sizes of hot and cold carts

Standard: Ensure all hot carts are clean before they are used and the heater is in good working order. Use the Sterno if the heater does not work. Hot carts must be hot (approx. 140+ degrees Fahrenheit/60+ degrees Celsius) and cold carts must be cold (approx. 32–40 degrees Fahrenheit/0-40 degrees Celsius).

Procedure

1. Ensure the various sizes of the carts are correct and appropriate for the food items for which they are to be used, as follows:
   • Small hot cart: holds sixty twelve-inch plated entrées or eighty-four eleven-inch plated appetizers
   • Large hot cart: holds ninety-six twelve-inch plated entrées or one hundred and twenty-eight eleven-inch plated appetizers
   • Vertical hot carts: for buffet foods
   • Cold carts: for cold buffet foods

Standards and Procedures
Job Title: Steward/Stewardess
Department: Stewarding

Task #39: Set up a hot cart
Standard: Check that the hot cart is hot and, if not, use Sterno. The temperature should be at least 140 degrees Fahrenheit (60 degrees Celsius).

Procedure

1. Know that the banquet steward will obtain a hot cart and bring it to the banquet kitchen.
2. Plug in the hot cart two hours before the function starts.
3. Get a dolly of the proper-sized plates, go through every plate, and check for chips, cracks, or dirty plates.
4. Add plate covers for every plate put into the hot cart.

Plates are heated separately in their dollies.

Standards and Procedures
Job Title: Steward/Stewardess
Department: Stewarding

Task #40: Know what to bring to a plate-up
Standard: Ensure all items needed for the plate-up are ready at the site at the time of plating-up.

Procedure

1. Bring the hot cart, plates, plate covers, and cleaning cloth to the plate-up.
   - Be sure the plates are hot.
   - Know how many plates are in the cart.
2. Ensure the cooks bring pitchers and spoons.
   - Ensure the pitchers for the sauce are correct and spoons are available for dishing up the foods.
   - Ensure the stewards bring clean cloths to wipe the plates.
   - Ensure everything is clean before use.
3. Take away all dirty spoons, pitchers, and hotel pans.
4. Ensure everything is cleaned up when the dish-up is over.

Standards and Procedures
Job Title: Steward/Stewardess
Department: Stewarding

Task #41: Set up and deliver soup
Standard: Warm soup cups and plates in a hot box two hours prior to service.

Procedure

Understand that soup is plated up two ways, depending on the service style of the function.

1. Standard Service
    *   Place soup cups or plates in the hot box to keep warm.
    *   Bring the hot box to the kitchen to be filled by the chef at the appropriate time.
    *   Deliver the soup to the dish-out station where the cups or plates are placed on the servers' trays.
2. French Service
    *   Place soup cups and a silver soup tureen in a hot box.
    *   Ensure there are two soup tureens plus covers for every table in the banquet.
    *   Deliver soup cups and tureens to the dish-up station empty.
    *   Take the pot of soup that the chef puts out to the dish-up station at the correct time (twenty minutes before serving).
    *   Ladle the soup into the tureens.
    *   Ensure the tureens are covered.
    *   Place the correct number of soup cups and saucers for the table on the servers' trays with a ladle.

Standards and Procedures
Job Title: Steward/Stewardess
Department: Stewarding

Task #42: Plate up and deliver salads

Standard: Ensure salads are delivered to the banquet kitchen thirty minutes prior to service time.

Procedure

1. Start the plate-up of salads immediately when informed by the chef.
2. Present the salad plates on oval trays.
3. Ensure the number of plates on the tray equals half the number of people seated per table, usually four or five.
4. Stack the trays on a Queen Mary.
5. Roll the salads to the location of the function.

Standards and Procedures
Job Title: Steward/Stewardess
Department: Stewarding

Task #43: Do plate-ups

Standard: Ensure all plates used for plate-ups are clean and in perfect condition with no chips, cracks, or scratches, and keep hot food in the hot box. Set up enough tables to plate all the dishes.

Procedure

1. Locate the dish-up (plate-up) area by the banquet prep area.
2. Obtain the hot cart, and take it to the dish-up area.
3. Ensure the banquet steward brings cleaning cloths, spoons, and pitchers when needed.
4. Set out the plates.
5. Take off the plate covers.
6. Turn the plate covers upside down at the end of the table next to the hot cart.
7. Ensure the banquet steward wipes clean the plates before the plate covers are put on.
8. Place the food on the plates.
9. Ensure the covers are placed over the food.
10. Stack plates on the trays.

Standards and Procedures
Job Title: Steward/Stewardess
Department: Stewarding

Task #44: Follow the banquet steward's checklist

Standard: Clean, sanitize, and put away all pots, pans, dishes, and utensils at the end of each shift.

Procedure

1. Check that your work area is clean, sanitized, neat, and organized while working and especially after the end of each shift.
2. Report broken equipment, low supplies, and accidents to the supervisor immediately.
3. Complete the following checklist after each function:
    a. Ensure that all glassware, china, and flatware is organized in the banquet hallway.
    b. Take all empty glass racks back to the stewarding area.
    c. Complete all setups and have them checked by a manager.
    d. Check all hot carts for old food.

Standards and Procedures
Job Title: Steward/Stewardess
Department: Stewarding

Task #45: Understand the night cleaner responsibilities
Standard: The night cleaner responsibilities are typically divided up by kitchen areas with one person responsible for the floors and the trash removal.

Procedure

1. Clean all the kitchens assigned to the night cleaner, including the equipment, floors, counters, and hoods.
2. Empty all trash cans.
3. Follow the monthly cleaning schedule, which includes ceilings, walk-in coolers, refrigerator gaskets, dish machines, and air vents.
4. Be informed by the supervisor which monthly duties will be assigned as your responsibilities.

Standards and Procedures
Job Title: Steward/Stewardess
Department: Stewarding

Task #46: Prepare for off-premise catering
Standard: Keep equipment and vehicles clean and sanitary.

Procedure

1. Check the catering equipment list.
2. Deliver the setup equipment to the site three hours before the function starts.
3. Deliver food to the event forty-five minutes before serving time.
4. Ensure the buffet setup is completed twenty minutes prior to serving the guests.
5. Set up a station for china, glasses and flatware, and so forth, with racks and carts.
6. Following closure of the buffet tables, remove the setup equipment, and reload on vehicles for return to the hotel.
7. Follow the catering checklist to make sure that items brought to the function are accounted for before leaving.
8. Report broken and missing equipment to the lead steward or manager.

Index

I

ice bath, 45
iodophor sanitizer, 51
iron stains, 31

K

keys, standards and procedures for
    checking out, 89

L

lead, 29
legionella, 29
lime deposits, 27–28
Listeria, 25
low-temperature gloves, 8

M

malodor, 45, 55, 109, 114
materials safety data sheets (MSDSs),
    17, 52
meats. *See* butcher shop
mercury, 29
mice, 59
microorganisms
    defined, 24
    found in water supplies, 29
    percent of as killed by sanitizers,
        40, 48
    use of chemical sanitizing to
        kill, 48
milk dispensers, standards and
        procedures for cleaning and
        sanitizing, 103
mold, 26
MSDSs (materials safety data sheets),
    17, 52

N

National Advisory Committee on
    Microbiological Criteria for
    Foods, 2
night cleaning, standards and
    procedures for, 134
nitrates, 29

O

Occupational Safety and Health
    Administration (OSHA), 51
off-premise catering, standards and
    procedures for, 135
ovens, standards and procedures for
    cleaning, 96

P

packaging, 34, 37
parasites, 29
pathogens, 24
personal hygiene, 18–21
personal protective equipment (PPE),
    9, 15, 31, 37, 47, 49
pesticides, 29
pests/pest control, 23, 37, 59–61
pH scale, 30
plate-ups, standards and procedures
    for, 129, 132
polishing duties, standards and
    procedures for, 122

Q

quaternary sanitizer (quats), 48, 50–51

R

racking, 56–58
ranges, standards and procedures for
    cleaning, 95
rats, 59, 63

temperature control for safety (TCS), 2–3

temperature danger zone (TDZ), 25, 43, 45, 64

thermometers, 43

three-compartment sink, 39–40

titrating of water, 28

total dissolved solids (TDS), 27, 28

toxoplasma, 29

U

uniforms, 9

US Environmental Protection Agency (EPA), 51, 62

V

vegetable bins, standards and procedures for cleaning, 106

vegetable peelers, standards and procedures for cleaning and sanitizing, 102

vibrio, 29

viruses, 25–26, 29

W

walk-in freezers, standards and procedures for cleaning, 105

wall charts

as guide at handwashing stations, 21

as guide for proper cleaning and sanitizing, 41, 42, 55

as guide to proper dispensation of chemical products, 52

walls, standards and procedures for cleaning, 98

warmers, 44

waste handling, 59–60, 62, 64

water

hardness of, 27–28

importance of, 27

potential contaminants in, 27, 28, 29

quality of, 27, 29, 31

titrating (testing) of, 28

water treatment, 29

water-softening system, 28–29

Wet Floor sign, 15

work preparation, standards and procedures for, 80–81

World Health Organization (WHO), 22, 23

Y

yeast, 26

Yersinia, 29